Do any of these apply

missing one of the main
ingredients.

*Y*ou forget your dental
appointment, but must
pay for the time slot
anyway.

*T*he kids neglect their
chores.

A new household item
needs repair, but you
can't remember when
the warranty expires.

*Y*ou forget a family
member's birthday.

*Y*ou'll be glad when
Christmas is over.

If you experience any
of these hassles, this
book is for you!

HOW TO TAKE THE HASSLE OUT OF HOME-MAKING

RENA STRONACH

LIVING BOOKS
Tyndale House
Publishers, Inc.
Wheaton, Illinois

Material in chapter 9 is taken from *Bernard Meltzer Solves Your Money Problems,* by Bernard Meltzer. Copyright 1982. Used by permission of Simon & Schuster, Inc.

Furniture pieces and floor-plan symbols in chapter 12 used by permission of Drexel and Heritage furniture company.

First printing, June 1986

Library of Congress Catalog Card Number 86-50012
ISBN 0-8423-1375-3

*This book
is dedicated
to my family,
who inspires
my best
homemaking
efforts.*

CONTENTS

PREFACE

Have you ever wished you could be a better Christian? Have you ever wished you could be like certain "great" people in the church? If someone were to ask you to list the qualities of a mature believer, what would you say?

You would probably suggest several things that "spiritual giants" have that you wish you possessed—a powerful prayer life, good character, strong Bible knowledge.

But one thing you might overlook, one thing that is at the foundation of Christian maturity, is the ability to make decisions and to act on them.

Let me explain. As Christians, our task on earth is to be faithful in a few things so that we will be *rulers* over many things in the world to come (Matt. 25:23). But any "ruling" is implementing a decision. To rule, then, is to evaluate a situation, decide on a course of action, and then *act*.

But, ironically, some Christians believe that being a good Christian means *not* deciding and *not* acting.

Take prayer, for instance. Some believers use prayer as an escape from making necessary decisions. Afraid to act on the situations, they decide to "let God handle them."

Other believers refuse to evaluate situations in their own lives because they are too painful. "Waiting on God" is easier, so the problems remain.

Of course, I do believe in prayer. I believe that miracles in my family have been brought about largely by my grandparents' prayers. I'll never forget their morning and evening prayers. I knew that prayer was a decision for them because, after they had invited their company to join in, they dropped to their knees regardless of who was present. So, yes, I believe that prayer is valuable and necessary.

But, isn't prayer more than a mere recitation of needs? Isn't it rather a response to our relationship with God? We know that every meaningful relationship requires trust by both parties. I trust God to give me wisdom about a situation, and he trusts me to use his wisdom to bring about change.

We know what would happen to a child if the parents made every decision for him. He would be crippled, and he would never become a responsible adult. Since God is raising sons, not robots, he leaves the decision making to us. He will never take over and raise our children for us. He will never strip us of our dignity.

This book is about gaining control over our

everyday lives. God wants us to rule in our lives now, for if we don't rule in the small decisions required every day, we probably don't rule at all.

My hope is that this book will help any woman who feels the need to bring more peace into her home by making wise, God-guided decisions.

INTRODUCTION
What Is a Hassle?

I'll never forget Amanda on the day of her wedding. She was like a storybook bride, full of joy and anticipation.

Amanda was a young woman who seemed destined for a successful life. She looked as if she could handle anything and had proven her abilities in college by graduating at the top of her class. She was intelligent, creative, and, above all, enthusiastic.

But I also cannot forget what I saw nine years later when I had lunch with Amanda. Her light-auburn hair framed the face of someone I hardly knew. She looked so much older. As we talked, I could tell that Amanda was tired, overworked, and unfulfilled. "You know, I feel as if I do nothing but yell at my kids anymore," she confessed. "I guess I wasn't cut out to be a mother."

Amanda was doing too much for any one person.

She was beginning to feel as though life were becoming just one big hassle.

Then there was Marge, a woman in her late thirties. Marge was more than just tired; she was nervous. She was finding it increasingly difficult to relax and enjoy the simple pleasures of life. Her nervousness was affecting her sleep, and her outlook on life was becoming overly negative.

"The other day my brother-in-law got on a joke-telling binge. I haven't laughed that hard in years," Marge volunteered. "It made me realize that I've almost forgotten how to laugh."

Marge was right. Most of the time she was too uptight to smile. She was just too busy coping with the everyday hassles in her personal life.

The word *hassle* is slang meaning "a state of confusion." If you are at all like Amanda or Marge, you aren't enjoying homemaking as you would like to because too many areas of your life are out of control, confused, and thus unfulfilling.

What are these hassles that plague so many homemakers? Hassles steal a woman's joy in living in two ways. The first way is through *small irritations,* when something gets out of order. These irritations can ruin even the best of days and cause tension in a woman's life. Below are a few typical small irritations. Check any that have happened to you.

☐ You begin cooking dinner and find you are missing one of the main ingredients.

- [ ] You forget your dental appointment, but must pay for the time slot anyway.
- [ ] Someone in your family can't find a clean pair of socks to wear.
- [ ] Your children are arguing a lot.
- [ ] The kids neglect their chores.
- [ ] The dog's license has expired, and you receive a fine from the animal control.
- [ ] A new household item needs repair, but you can't remember when the warranty expires.
- [ ] You want to return a new item of clothing, but can't find the sales slip.
- [ ] You forget a family member's birthday.
- [ ] You forget to write an excuse for your child's absence from school.

A hassle of the second kind is less obvious and therefore more devastating. It can go unsolved for years. We know the hassle is there, but we can't lay a finger on its source. The Christmas season for some women is a prime example of this type of hassle.

Christmastime is frustrating for many people, but women in particular have difficulty because they usually have much added work during the holidays. They cook, decorate, shop, and entertain. But they also anticipate family closeness and even spiritual renewal during the celebration of Christ's birth.

But many women still admit, "I'll be glad when Christmas is over." Why? These women are probably tired and maybe disappointed that they didn't experience as much Christmas joy as they wanted.

Why should it be that way? Why should we spend that month every year bringing on ourselves more stress than enjoyment? Why don't we change the way we handle Christmas? If we removed the hassles, we could avoid being too tired to enjoy the close family times.

Throughout the year, however, other less-apparent hassles affect us psychologically and spiritually. Check any of these that apply to you.

- ☐ You find little time or energy to do things with the kids.
- ☐ You find housework a drudgery.
- ☐ You feel overly obligated to outside activities.
- ☐ You seldom take time for personal interests.
- ☐ You have a hard time concentrating on what family members say to you.
- ☐ You overeat due to boredom.
- ☐ You sense no family closeness at dinnertime.
- ☐ You aren't excited about decorating the house as you once were.
- ☐ You worry a lot about money.
- ☐ You feel that entertaining is more trouble than it's worth.

If you experience any of these hassles, this book is for you. Even the smallest hassles merit attention because they can detract from our service to Christ.

Perhaps you would like to bring new meaning, enjoyment, and ease to your homemaking. The following chapters provide a workable plan for bringing about change in your home.

The first step shown is how to slow down and get off the merry-go-round so that your mind can be the

creative tool it was designed to be. Second, two kinds
of planning are adapted from the business world for
use in your home. The first one is macro-planning,
which is the overall plan, and the second one is
micro-planning, which keeps things working day by
day.

Then these principles are *applied* to nine specific
areas of homemaking. Finally, I discuss how to keep
sane in spite of hassles. Hassles will indeed come and
go, but two things will enable you to master them:
time spent alone doing things you enjoy, and time
spent with God.

PART ONE: MAKE YOUR PLAN

ONE
Stopping the Merry-Go-Round

It is sad that most people think they have too little time for the things they want to do. I believe the truth is that we all have time for the things we consider most important. The trouble is that we allow ourselves to become involved in too many activities. We don't need more time, but we do need more courage to invest the time we have in the things we value most highly.

TIME OUT

A major reason that a person's life becomes too hectic is the inability to think creatively. Perhaps you have experienced this. You lack mental energy. You barely function day after day. Your mind isn't at its best; it's tired and overloaded.

The modern woman is especially susceptible to this merry-go-round syndrome. Today, 6 out of 10 mothers with young children are either working or looking for work. In America, 50 million women work outside of the home. More than ever, they need the ability to think clearly and creatively.

But fitting too many activities into your time can do more than just dull your creative thinking. Stress can damage your body. High blood pressure, illness, lethargy, anxiety, and inability to enjoy people and things are only a few of the penalties that befall the person who takes on too many obligations and ideals. This often happens to a woman. She ends up losing the joy and fulfillment of being a homemaker.

When you start your campaign to become a hassle-free homemaker, you must first take some time out to reflect. How much reflection is needed depends on the individual. If your life is extremely busy, you will probably need more than one short session.

I find it helpful to set aside a certain block of time for reflection, say two weeks. During that time, I slow down as much as possible so I can think. It takes a while for me to become stubborn enough to refuse invitations and opportunities and dedicate this time to myself. But during such times, I can feel my mind becoming more alert and creative.

Early in my marriage I was forced to take several months away from my fast-paced American way of life. I joined my husband in a small town in Germany where he was stationed in the service. Our German landlady taught me one of the most important lessons of my life.

One day before dinner, she and I were walking the

mile to the small village. A small-featured woman, Frau Welsch leaned over to pick up a walking stick for me. Then she looked over her small, rimmed glasses and said, "You must walk, Rena, every day. It's good for you and the baby."

I was pregnant with our first child, and Frau Welsch felt was it her personal responsibility to do for me what any good mother would do for her daughter. Since my mother was back in the States, Frau Welsch insisted that I take up the daily walks to which the people there were accustomed. And walk we did— every day!

I'll never forget the day—probably because I was eight months pregnant—that we climbed the mountainside to visit a shepherd's home. The old, white-bearded man was shearing, but he stopped long enough to call out the names of several of his sheep. We listened to their *baas* in response.

That day I learned a vivid lesson about Christ the Shepherd as I watched that old shepherd call his sheep by name. I also learned another lesson: life is far richer if you slow down a little to think.

Why not set aside some time and dedicate it to yourself? Make the courageous decision to get off the merry-go-round for a while. Would anything bad happen? Probably not. When you take some time out to reflect, you begin your campaign to take the hassles out of your homemaking duties so that you can more fully enjoy your home, your family, and yourself.

As you develop your plan, keep in mind the following guidelines.

ORGANIZATION

Many hassles come through lack of organization. Maybe when you hear the word *organization,* you instantly think of more work. After all, doesn't getting organized mean you keep a perfect house? No! To organize means to harmonize the different areas of your life into one balanced whole.

You already know the numerous duties for which the average homemaker is responsible: the house, children, a marriage, money, pets, and maybe a career. Note that housekeeping is only one of these areas. If you are truly organized, you will not place undue emphasis on any one area. You will need to do less work, not more, in some areas so you can keep a watchful eye on all of your responsibilities.

Bringing organization to your home requires sensitivity to your family members. You could be an immaculate housekeeper, yet be insensitive to your bored child who needs some direction. So if you aren't the ideal housekeeper, don't lose heart. Ask yourself, Am I sensitive to my own needs and to the needs of my family? If you think you are, then you will find getting organized much easier than you may have thought.

PURPOSE

Your purpose in life comes from believing that your role as woman is an important one. We know our earthly roles are temporary, because in God's eternal kingdom our responsibilities will be different. But our assignments in the new kingdom will depend greatly on our having taken our present assignments seriously. Your assignment as a homemaker, therefore, should be tackled with the same seriousness of purpose as any other given on earth.

When I realized that my lifelong apprenticeship on earth is necessary training for God's purposes, I quit asking God for more and different responsibilities and began to earnestly fulfill those he had already given me.

Can you see beyond the mundane, seemingly unimportant tasks you must do? Can you do these tasks as unto the Lord until your life here is over? You can if first you realize that the best way for you to be trained for important things is to take personal responsibility for small things. By being courageous in these small duties, you may never receive much praise from people. But God will know that you did your best.

COMMITMENT

To commit yourself means to decide you are worthy to succeed at what you do. A life of fulfillment will never happen accidentally. True fulfillment doesn't have as much to do with things and events as it has to do with knowing that you have succeeded in what you consider important.

Of course, as human beings our ultimate worth and

dignity come from our decision to allow Christ's death to bring us forgiveness and salvation. Christians know that no one can place a value on himself that surpasses the value God places on him. But remember: the value of anything is based on the price paid by the purchaser. And the greatest price in creation was paid for you and me. Therefore, the value of each life should never be questioned. Relax in God's love and believe that you deserve an abundant, joyful life.

As you take time out in the weeks you have chosen, make a fresh commitment before the God who made you. Then resolve to take control of the several areas of your life for your own pleasure and for his. As you do this, you will gain the fulfillment you deserve.

PLANNING

A plan is a course of action you lay out after you have evalutated your situation. The next two chapters are about developing the skill of planning, but for now, consider this: Planning is the difference between being in control of your circumstances and being controlled by them.

Being in control means you are no longer just hoping things will turn out right. You are no longer just a spectator wishing for changes. Instead, you are taking active steps toward becoming a part of the solution. A woman who plans gains confidence because she is actively involved in her areas of concern. She has a step-by-step course of action to help her succeed in her duties.

Planning is the way you implement the organization to which you have committed yourself. Planning is essential, and it works!

▶CHAPTER AT A GLANCE

1. *Time Out:* Take time away from your daily activities so that you can think creatively.
2. *Organization:* Balance your workload. You need to work less, not more.
3. *Purpose:* Recognize the importance of your role as woman.
4. *Commitment:* Make a pact before God to lead an abundant life with dignity and peace.
5. *Planning:* Chart your course of action for success.

TWO
Macro-planning: The Overall Plan

What would happen if a business executive arrived at work one day with no plan of action? Suppose she set aside all goals and business procedures and employed no planning. Suppose she operated totally on a contingency basis. Very soon, she would be out of business.

In any endeavor, good management requires adherence to some basic principles. Whether you are the president of a bank, the manager of a retail clothing store, or manager of the homefront, you will find that some fundamental planning principles can provide direction and produce results.

Perhaps you have never thought of yourself as a manager. But the word *executive,* or *manager,* simply means "one who gives direction or takes charge." As a modern woman, your various roles require good planning skills every day. So why not learn to manage your life as top-level executives manage their businesses? A successful business manager would not violate basic management principles, so why should you?

Of course there are differences between the home manager and the business executive. Unlike the executive, the homemaker is not a hired employee. She punches no time clock; she receives no monthly paycheck; and she has no yearly evaluations or board of directors to whom she must report.

The consequences of poor planning, however, are the same for both: disorder, confusion, communication breakdown, loss of profits, poor morale, unused talent, and poor productivity. Also, the payoffs of good leadership are the same: order, clear direction, specific modes of operation, open communication, increased profits, pleasant working environment, good morale, and creative and productive coworkers. Why is it then that some women find it difficult to manage their homes?

One important reason is that they lack confidence in their managerial abilities. They should note, however, that the Bible designates the woman as home manager (Prov. 31). Every woman does have the basic skills necessary to perform her job. But she needs to learn to approach any hassle the same way professionals do.

GUIDELINES FOR MACRO-PLANNING
To learn how business professionals manage hassles, I undertook a study of how they succeed in business. I

interviewed people at business consulting firms, and I read numerous books about managerial success. These efforts were very fruitful. I developed guidelines that should help you determine your management strategies.

Write it down. You need to prepare and work from a written plan. In his book *Entrepreneuring*, Steven Brandt puts it this way: "There is powerful evidence that the act of committing an idea to paper is a vital step in its development."

Writing your plan on paper seems elementary, doesn't it? Can't we simply remember such things? You may be interested in knowing that even Albert Einstein resorted to notetaking. He did his thinking on paper. Psychologists tell us that 83 to 87 percent of everything that comes into the brain comes through the eyes. Thus, when you write your plan on paper and review it from time to time, you will not likely forget it.

When you sit down to plan with pencil and paper, you will be squarely facing an issue, perhaps for the first time. Writing helps you crystallize matters in your mind. Seeing a hassle on paper eliminates the vagueness that leads a person to remain passive and uninvolved. Somehow, once your problem is clearly stated, you can more easily accept the responsibility for eliminating it.

Keep it simple. As you make your plan, remember to keep it simple. A spokesman for Texas Instruments says it this way: "More than two objectives is no objectives." When he took over at Dana, Rene McPherson threw out twenty-two-and-a-half inches of policy manuals. He replaced them with a one-page statement of the company's philosophy.

In other words, even some big companies realize that the human mind is simply incapable of holding more than five or six ideas at a time. Success comes as we accomplish our objectives. Therefore, a macro-plan must be simple both for clarity and to allow for human limitations.

Be flexible. After you have made your plan, maintain flexibility. In their book *In Search of Excellence,* Thomas S. Peters and Robert W. Waterman, Jr., write: "As the needs of their customers shift, the skills of their competitors improve, the mood of the public perturbates, . . . these companies tack, revamp, adjust, transform and adapt . . . they innovate." Most big business planners would agree.

A plan is helpful only if you are able to adjust it, change it, or even throw it out altogether and make a new one. You and your family are always in a state of change. As the kids grow up, your financial status varies, or your needs change, so must your plan.

Listen to your family. Good listening is essential for good planning. Make a habit of listening to your family so you will know what they need. Sam Walton is the force behind Wal-Mart. He took the company's worth from $45 million to $1.6 billion in the 1970s. According to a story in *The Wall Street Journal:* "Mr. Walton couldn't sleep a few weeks back. He got up and bought four dozen doughnuts at an all-night bakery. At 2:30 A.M., he took them to a distribution center and chatted for a while with workers from the docks."

The point is that Mr. Walton cared about his twenty-six thousand employees. He says, "The key is to get out into the store and listen to what the associates [employees] have to say."

As a homemaker, you must remember that your plans almost always involve the people in your family. And, of course, the whole reason for developing plans is to make your lives better. Listen to the complaint and suggestions of each family member so your plans will be appropriate.

Try something. A plan that is not implemented is not really a plan at all. "But above all try something," said Franklin D. Roosevelt.

If you see a hassle and write a plan to eliminate it, then you must follow through until the problem is solved. Stubborn persistence is worth its weight in gold. Implementing your plan is the difference between being an amateur and being a professional. Put action behind your words, or you'll have no results. Waiting for something to happen by itself is like waiting for a flower to come up in the spring when you never planted any seeds in the first place.

Pay attention to details. Minding details is especially necessary in the day-to-day planning we shall discuss in the next chapter. But whatever our level of planning, the greatest success is achieved when we give attention to the details that other people may overlook.

Ray Kroc, founder of McDonald's, said, "I emphasize the importance of details. You must perfect every fundamental of your business if you expect it to perform well." One McDonald's employee talked about the details of his training. During the first few weeks of training, he moved from one level of food preparation to the next. McDonald's break room had instructional TV and cassettes going all the time, stressing one aspect or another of proper McDonald's procedures. McDonald's spells out each detail: "Cooks must turn, never flip, hamburgers. If they haven't been purchased, Big Macs must be discarded ten minutes after being cooked, and french fries in seven minutes. Cashiers must always make eye contact with and smile at every customer." McDonald's has been so successful for all these years because of attention to detail.

Evaluate your plan. Evaluation times are essential but need not be complicated. Pick a time each week that you can glance at your written plan (Sunday works for me). It might take only a few seconds to remind yourself and keep on track. While evaluation times need not adhere to a rigid schedule, you may also want to include monthly and quarterly checkpoints. The purpose of evaluation is to see how things are going, to see if your plan should be modified, or to see if it is completed.

HOW TO MAKE YOUR PLAN

Make a goal statement. To begin developing any kind of plan, you must ask yourself an important question: What do I want? Let me illustrate with an example from my own experience. During our children's early grade-school years, I began organizing their chores using lists. I was so anxious to make sure they did their chores that I forgot why I had delegated them in the first place. I was always reminding the children to do their tasks. Noticing this, my husband took me aside one day and asked, "Why do we give the kids household responsibilities anyway?" I stopped short because I hadn't thought nearly as much about the *why* as I had the *how* of getting the children to do their chores. We decided that the purpose of chores was to instill responsibility rather than to merely "get the garbage out."

After our talk, I knew I must quit giving verbal reminders. I had to allow each child to think for himself. After a day or two without listening to records (their favorite pastime), they did begin carrying out their responsibilities.

Until you decide what you really want to accomplish, you won't be directing your energies most effectively. Choose a specific area of your homemaking duties and decide what changes you want. Then make a goal statement. This goal statement is your ultimate objective for the changes you want to accomplish in this area.

Implement the four steps of planning. No matter what terms you use, making a plan involves these four things: (1) your goal—choose your ultimate objective; (2) the problem—define your particular hassle; (3) the barriers—identify what stands in the way of solving the matter; and (4) your solution—select specific actions to eliminate the hassle exactly.

Here is an example of how we overcame a minor hassle in our household.

Trying to get five people out of the house each morning was becoming quite tense. We discovered, however, that the tension was coming from some avoidable little irritants. Each morning, both parents and three teenage children wanted to shower and blow-dry their hair. So some of us occupied the bathrooms for long periods of time while others were kept waiting. We all took turns using the one good hair dryer. Consequently, we were often late getting out the door, and sometimes the kids were leaving without breakfast.

This is not an uncommon problem for many households. The solution is easy, but it's helpful to illustrate how it looks on paper.

We posted this plan on our refrigerator so that we could all be involved. Using this simple procedure, we easily eliminated our morning tensions. By tackling our hassle head-on, we brought greater peace to our home. We gained confidence in eliminating a small

GOAL	Peace in the morning, the family on time, everyone eating breakfast.
PROBLEM	Only one hair dryer, run out of hot water, kids missing breakfast, late for school and work.
BARRIERS	Money (for hair dryers), time, space, cooperation.
SOLUTION	Buy two more hair dryers (one per month), schedule two evening showers, get up fifteen minutes earlier to allow time for breakfast.

hassle and prevented it from becoming larger later on.

Do you have a hassle in your home right now? Use the steps of plan development to solve the hassle you are facing. Take the time to write in the space provided on the following page.

Use your calendar. Once you have identified a hassle in your home and have written a plan of action, use your monthly calendar to decide when you will implement your plan. Choose one day this week to begin and write it on your calendar. Be sure to set aside times for each step of the plan and for evaluation. Also choose an approximate time for the completion of your plan.

Continue to mark on your calendar until it becomes

GOAL

_____

PROBLEM

_____

BARRIERS

_____

SOLUTION

_____

a habit. And treat each step on the calendar as you
would a dental appointment: *keep it*. Don't be
distracted!

Developing an overall plan is absolutely necessary
before you begin day-to-day planning. It will help
you meet goals rather than just keep up with daily
demands. Then your day-to-day planning will help you
implement your overall plans. Remember, a woman
with a plan is one who can bring direction to her
home and to her life.

►CHAPTER AT A GLANCE
  1. Write it down.
  2. Keep it simple.

3. Be flexible.
4. Listen to your family.
5. Try something.
6. Pay attention to details.
7. Evaluate your plan.
8. Make a goal statement.
9. Implement the four steps of planning.
   a. goal
   b. problem
   c. barriers
   d. solution
10. Use your calendar.

THREE
Micro-planning:
The Details

Stewardship in the Bible refers to stewardship of one day at a time. Handling each day to the best of our abilities is the challenge set before us.

How many great things have you accomplished in the past five years? You are probably like me: You may not be able to think of any great things you have done. Most of us lead ordinary lives filled with the ordinary happenings of daily living. From my perspective, I think that is the way a Christian's life is supposed to be.

As Christians we know our destiny is a great one because we are being prepared for roles in the kingdom of God. So while we lead our lives with an eye toward our heavenly future, we must deal responsibly with our present human existence.

You can imagine how Christ must have felt while he lived on earth. He knew his destiny and his identity, yet he knew his humanity also. Jesus spent the first thirty years of his life as a member of a family and as a carpenter. Then he had three years of intensive ministry, but died without fully revealing all of his glory. That is postponed until his second coming.

So what does this have to do with day-to-day planning? Here is the connection: Life is mostly ordinary living, but it is lived in the promise of our heavenly future. Every day we face the challenge of a normal day with its normal duties. We succeed or fail according to our fulfillment of daily responsibilities.

The ways in which we conduct our everyday affairs produce one of two results: order or chaos. And chaos is the breeding ground for discouragement, confusion, and even depression. It can ruin the whole day. Much worse, it distracts us from Christ. To achieve order in our lives, we must decide to take control of each day before it arrives.

Eliminate backtracking. Joyce used to spend much of her time backtracking. One day a while back she spent twenty minutes looking for a clean pair of socks that her first-grader, Jeff, could wear to school. Because of Joyce's search for socks, breakfast was late, Jeff missed the school bus, and she and her son got into an argument. As Joyce drove Jeff to school, she felt guilty for the harsh words that had been spoken between them. While Jeff was in class, he had a hard time concentrating on his lessons.

Running errands later in the day, Joyce forgot to buy one of the ingredients for the evening meal. That forced her to spend thirty extra frustrating minutes going back to the grocery store.

Consequently, Joyce spent about seventy minutes of her busy day in time-consuming backtracking. It cost her (1) a harmonious morning with her son; (2) getting started on that special project; (3) extra gasoline money; and (4) most important of all, peace of mind.

If your day resembles Joyce's, you may not realize that only ten minutes of daily planning can spare you hours of unnecessary work. Not only can planning save you time and energy, but it can save you a lot of frustration as well. Here is how a daily, ten-minute planning session works.

Keep a monthly calendar. Think of your calendar as a tourist thinks of his road map. It will show you where you have been and where you are going. At the beginning of each month, mark these items on the appropriate days: birthdays, medical and dental appointments, business engagements, hair appointments, family outings, and dinner plans. I also use my calendar to designate time for exercising, meeting special goals, and having leisurely dinners with the family.

After you have prepared your calendar for the upcoming month, you are ready to spend just ten minutes each day to keep your life running smoothly.

Write a daily to-do list. You may have an excellent memory. However, you will inevitably forget some things if you rely only on your memory. The varied roles the modern woman plays can make life quite complicated. Your memory won't be able to keep all of the small daily details in order. So, think out these details on paper just as you do for overall planning.

Organize your activities by making a to-do list for the upcoming day. This type of list is widely used in the business world. Ask any successful business person how he or she keeps track of daily tasks. You will probably learn that their productivity results from paying attention to and writing down small details so they will not be forgotten.

By simply writing your plan for the next day on paper, you will probably experience an uncluttering of your mind. You can then concentrate on more creative endeavors since, with your daily tasks listed, you don't need to spend energy trying to remember them. You can easily review them the next morning.

Essentially, the list is an extension of your calendar. When you make your list, write high priority items at the top of the page and low priority items at the bottom. Items given top priority should be those that require immediate attention, while low-priority items can be done, if necessary, on a less harried day.

Now review your monthly calendar to see what you have scheduled for tomorrow. As you write your daily to-do list, be sure to include the items on your calendar. You can carry your list wherever you go to remind you of what to do next.

Suppose tomorrow's schedule looks like this:

11:00 Joey's shot
12:00 Ladies' luncheon
 5:30 Sally and Jim for dinner

Now consider the several steps that are necessary to accomplish these three items:

TO-DO LIST

High priority items:
   Take meat out of freezer
   Lay out shot record
   Bake cake for dinner
   Buy gasoline for the car
   11:00 Joey's shot
   12:00 Ladies' luncheon
   Buy dinner napkins
   Cook dinner
   5:30 Sally and Jim for dinner

Low priority items:
   Color hair
   Dust furniture

Save time by doing several tasks at once. Having listed the things you should do tomorrow, look over the next few days of your monthly calendar. Is there something else you could do tomorrow that will save you time later on? Perhaps Joey's birthday is coming up in a couple of days. While you are out buying the dinner napkins, you could buy birthday party supplies. Add that to your list. It may help you to organize your to-do lists a week at a time. When you think of something you need to do later in the week, write it down on the list for the appropriate day so that you don't have to think about it again. Then each evening, review and complete the list for the following day.

Attend to high priority items first, and if you still have time, begin the less important tasks. Some days your list may be only half finished, while other days you will have extra time to begin tasks that need to be completed later in the week. Complete each item before moving on to the next, and then check it off your list. This will give you a satisfying feeling of accomplishment.

Get ready for the next day in advance. Each evening your daily to-do list should take about five minutes to complete. During the remaining five minutes of your ten-minute planning session, you work to get ready for the upcoming day.

Each person's needs and habits are different. I don't function at my best early in the morning, so I need extra help during those few minutes before I leave for work. That is why I use my remaining five minutes to pack everyone's lunches, except for the perishables, the night before. While I pack the lunches, I plan our dinner menu for the next day and transfer any frozen meat I will need from the freezer to the refrigerator. Then I give the laundry a last-minute check. If a load is finished in the dryer, I quickly sort it, putting each family member's clothes in a neat pile for them to fold. I also encourage each child to lay out his own clothes the night before.

If you work nonstop for those five minutes, you will be surprised how much you can accomplish in so short a time. Your daily ten-minute planning strategy will help you have a smooth-running tomorrow. You can use the time you save to work on a favorite hobby or read a good book. However you spend your newfound free time, you will feel more in control. You will be running your life; it won't be running you ragged.

The to-do list is a wonderful tool, but what do you do if you sit down to write your list for the next day and you have almost nothing to write? Rejoice! You have a slow day that can be put to good use. Of course, it is easy to coast for a while, and for certain days that may be just what the doctor ordered. However, doing things in advance is how most women are able to be productive.

A slow day is a wonderful opportunity. You can prepare for an upcoming hectic day. You can begin neglected projects or get a head start on future projects. Slow times are perfect for deep housecleaning that gets done only once or twice each year. You can clean out a closet or cupboard, or you may want to scrub some of the walls to remove fingerprints. On a slow day you can bake goods to be put in the freezer for future needs. During slow times I do most of my overall planning, financial planning, vacation planning, or holiday planning.

What do you do on those days when your to-do list seems endless? Go ahead and write down everything you need to do. Here is where prioritizing helps. Do not start any low-priority tasks unless you have finished all the important items.

During hectic times, I try to remember that I am human and have a limit as to how much I can accomplish. Some things must be saved for another day. I may need to plan better next time. I also consider any outside resources available to me. Maybe I could call a friend for help or use commercial resources. For instance, I could let the cleaners replace a zipper in a pair of pants instead of doing it myself. Sometimes I let the bakery do my baking.

Keep motivated. The one disadvantage of daily micro-planning is that is it always needed. A lifetime may entail more than twenty-five thousand days for which to plan. How does one remain motivated so that this daily stewardship is not neglected? I use three motivators.

The first is the *five-minute motivator.* If I find myself stalling or neglecting any task, I determine to invest just five short minutes. I am always surprised at how much I can accomplish in only five minutes. Even if I only arrange the needed supplies, five minutes is a beginning. I don't mind giving some task those few minutes. But if I had to give thirty minutes, I would probably never get started. And quite often, once I begin with my five-minute motivator, I become willing to work longer!

The second motivator is *instant rewards.* If I am having trouble staying motivated, I spend my five minutes and then give myself a reward, something I have been wanting to do. An instant reward can be almost anything: a beauty appointment, a long soak in the bathtub, a concert, a good book, a new dinner recipe. It is anything I give myself just to be nice to myself. Even buying a gallon of paint may motivate me to keep the house better. Don't feel guilty about rewards. It is good business to keep motivated.

The third motivator is *goal reviews*. These are simply quiet times when I reflect on my overall plans. These important plans can too easily fade into the background. Still, these are really of utmost importance to me. As I glance again at my written plans, even for only a few minutes, I find new energy and new commitment to keep going. I encourage myself not to settle for the mediocre. I challenge myself to strive for better things.

Micro-planning is a simple thing to do, but it is the "nuts and bolts" of any operation. It is what makes the operation great. Small and seemingly insignificant details are easy to overlook. Yet any business or family success comes from paying attention to the little things that accomplish the overall goals. Day-to-day planning will bring you success in everything you do because it brings results. It transfers our intentions into "shoe leather."

▶CHAPTER AT A GLANCE
1. Eliminate backtracking.
2. Keep a monthly calendar.

3. Write a daily to-do list.
4. Save time by doing several tasks at once.
5. Get ready for the next day in advance.
6. Keep motivated.

FOUR
Establishing Priorities

You make priority decisions every day. Just this morning, if you prepared breakfast, you knew which food items had to receive your first attention to have the complete meal ready by breakfast time.

Let's suppose that tonight you decide to violate the normal laws of cooking and declare that all of your menu is equal; no part deserves prior attention. At four o'clock, you put every item to be baked in the oven at once: the turkey, rolls, potatoes, and dressing. You know what kind of dinner you will serve (or, rather, won't be able to serve!) to your guests. When the rolls are ready, the turkey will be just beginning to bake. By the time the turkey is ready, the rest of the dinner will be burnt to a crisp.

Knowing which item needs attention first is choosing priorities—taking several items and arranging them in order of importance. A priority item gets first claim on your attention.

That makes establishing priorities sound simple, doesn't it? Priority planning encompasses every area of a woman's life, but sometimes issues and decisions are not as simple as cooking a meal. Sometimes prioritizing requires difficult, spur-of-the-moment decision making. Below are four humorous caricatures of women who are poor prioritizers. The elements of truth in their lives can help women become better decision makers.

Injudicious Jane. Jane has such good intentions. But she is so busy listening to others that she doesn't know what she herself believes or wants. Every morning Jane listens to Christian broadcasting. Every Tuesday afternoon she attends a ladies' Bible study. Both of these are wonderful, but Jane listens to so many voices, tapes, books, sermons, and TV programs that she does very little thinking or decision making of her own. She believes that only other people's opinions matter. Just about the time her focus turns to an area of need in her home, she hears another message that influences her to change her direction. She has not realized that her own ideas deserve as much consideration as anyone else's.

Flighty Florence. Florence has many talents. She begins project after project, but seldom finishes any of them. She gets the kids excited about a new family program, but before anyone gets started, Florence has forgotten about it. Her cupboards could produce such things as an uncompleted chore list for the kids (it lasted one week), a forgotten note about enrolling the kids in a youth activity, and an unused menu. Florence is going nowhere fast. She would do well to slow down, begin one thing, and finish it.

Insecure Ida. Ida is famous for doing nothing because she doesn't know what she should be doing. It is much easier to let things slide, allowing someone else to take the responsibility. That way Ida doesn't have to risk the consequences of a wrong decision. The trouble is that every day Ida suffers the consequences of her passivity. Her household hassles are multiplying, and so Ida feels more and more inadequate and insecure. Ida needs to make a decision—any decision—even if it doesn't work out.

Helpful Hannah. Hannah spends her best energy helping people other than her family. Most people think Hannah is wonderful. The only problem is that Hannah's priorities are unclear. If you ask her what she cares about the most, she insists it's her family. But Hannah feels such a need to help other people that she neglects herself and the people she loves most. Hannah's call to help others must be balanced with a realization that she is not the savior of the world; only Jesus can fulfill that office.

DEVELOP DECISION-MAKING SKILLS
Every woman must become comfortable in making her own decisions. In fact, it is dangerous to allow anyone

else to make your decisions because you are ultimately responsible for your own actions. Still, some women abdicate even small decisions to others. They passively allow hassles to remain, expecting other family members to take control and work toward a solution.

There are other types of people who allow even important personal decisions to be made by someone else. Religious cults are filled with people who have abandoned reliance on their own thinking and have accepted the leadership of unwise but confident-sounding leaders. An extreme example of people (many of them educated) who abandoned their own decision making was the well-known Jonestown incident. Hundreds of people committed simultaneous suicide at the command of Jim Jones. Why? They were following and believing in another human being instead of trusting their own judgment.

Why is decision making so difficult for some women? We have no easy answer, but two things deserve consideration as potential stumbling blocks. These can hinder even mundane, everyday decision making. Thus a woman's ability to establish priorities and follow a plan to eliminate hassles in the home becomes impossible.

Christians can be assertive. Some women believe Christians must be passive, and that assertiveness is somehow wrong. And choosing priorities is an assertive action that requires a yes or no judgment. Many Christian women feel guilty if they are not available to respond to any area of need. And I suppose, if we looked only at certain verses of the Bible to the exclusion of others, we could come to that conclusion. There are verses in the Bible that teach people to turn the other cheek and to walk two miles if anyone asks them to walk one mile. However, if you try to apply only these verses to every situation, you will probably have a very distorted, unrealistic view of Christianity. Christ also taught that "if your brother offends you, rebuke him," and by example Christ taught us to assert ourselves. Many times, Christ forthrightly answered people who were manipulating him, trying to change his course of action. Sometimes it is even wrong to turn the other cheek and not deal with a situation.

A Christian woman must learn to assert her prerogatives when it comes to choosing priorities. She must remember that Christ was the most humble, submissive man who ever lived. Yet he still made decisions and said no to some people. I love the example in Mark 11:27-33. The religious leaders came to Jesus with the question, "By what authority are you doing these things?" Jesus answered by asking if they believed the baptism of John was from heaven or from men. Jesus knew that the scribes and elders would be unable to answer his question honestly because they wanted to please the people. So Christ also refused to answer their question. Jesus never felt obligated to believe as others wished him to. Consequently, he was able to do God's will.

You and I must acquire the very normal, Christian

ability to choose what is best for ourselves and for our families. Then we must act on our decisions. What works for others will not necessarily work for you. Even your pastor may have a particular insight into raising kids that may not work for you. You have to decide as you seek God's guidance and use your own ability to reason.

Good decision making is based on absolutes.
Some women feel guilty or narrow-minded when making decisions if they insist that certain things are right or wrong. If you are forty years of age or younger, you have grown up in an era in which many people believe there are no absolutes. Being broadminded is regarded as intellectual, and saying something is right or wrong is considered backward. All ethical decisions are seen as relative and situational.

Modern thinking has abandoned the foundation of reason upon which it relied in past ages. That foundation necessitated people's trust that human reason can discover absolute truth. Take Isaac Newton, a great thinker of the 1600s. He discovered laws of motion that are foundational to physics because he believed in three things: (1) the universe has an innate orderliness, (2) an Orderer sustains the universe, and (3) truth is absolute.

Recent modern thinkers who hold atheistic views seem to grasp instinctively that faith in an orderly universe and absolute truth lead inevitably to the acknowledgment of an orderly Supreme Being. Therefore, they developed a system of reasoning that views the universe in a way that does not need absolute truth, nor an Orderer.

The Christian viewpoint is not threatened by true laws of reason. Christians know that an Orderer created our orderly universe. Thus, we know that absolute truth can guide us toward discovering the purpose of our existence. We must not be intimidated by reasoning that leads us away from belief in our own power to reason.

Consider how modern thinking applies to ethics. Lunacy is treated as correct and moral certitude as foolish. One example of this is the issue of abortion. A child's right to live is questioned even when the health of the mother is not jeopardized. Fortunately, Christians are not left alone with their own reasoning when we consider such issues. We have revealed truth in Scripture upon which to base our views.

Modern thinking has lost sight of the Creator and thus has fostered moral passivity. That is how healthy decision making is undermined. Without a Creator, your life has no ultimate purpose. You merely exist and wonder if your efforts and choices really matter. Modern thinking does not undermine any specific decision; it undermines decision making as a whole. But if you believe in a Creator, then you know that life has a purpose. God wants you to be a steward over all that you have, and this requires that you make daily decisions.

Simply stated, making decisions is right, not wrong. God does not despise choices; he encourages you to make them and to take charge of your day. Don't worry about making mistakes. Remember that the decisions we make on earth are training for our future assignments in heaven.

Learn to say no. Choosing priorities requires you to say yes to some things and no to others. Do not feel guilty even if, for the sake of your chosen commitments, you turn down some of the most noble opportunities for Christian service. Only you know what is best in your own situation. To acquire confidence in this area, we must practice saying no to people. Here are some helpful phrases to use if you need help saying no:

> "Thanks for the invitation, but I have already made other plans."
> "I am flattered that you would ask me to hold that position on the committee, but I have some things right now that require extra attention. Thanks for asking." (You never need to explain why you cannot accept. People don't usually expect to be told your private affairs, and you shouldn't feel obligated to fill in all the details if someone is inclined to pry.)
> "Could I call you back on this? I need to check my schedule." (You are wise to think about the consequences before you give an answer.)

Remember that hassles are strongly associated with the failure to establish priorities and stick to them. Making priority decisions brings order to your life.

In your home, do you sense the need for strong priority planning? Do you have needs that require your attention right now? Do you have distractions that are getting in your way?

Take a moment to list the items that need your priority attention:

1.
2.
3.
4.
5.

Now list the distractions that prevent you from paying attention to these needs:

1.
2.
3.
4.
5.

Now try to eliminate the distractions so you can take care of your priority items right away.

Be a smart prioritizer. Let's consider a woman who knows how to establish priorities and follow through on them. She finds it easy to relax. She works at a sensible pace because she knows what she wants to do. She feels comfortable making decisions. An event doesn't distract her; it only influences her priority planning when she finds that the event is beneficial to her situation. She begins projects and sticks to them until they are completed. She is secure about who she is and what she needs to do. Because she is not afraid to make mistakes, she learns from them. When she helps people, she keeps her helping in balance with other responsibilities and personal needs. She feels comfortable saying "no, thank you." By doing this she can say yes to the priorities Christ has given her. Best of all, she is growing as a person and is seeing the fulfillment of her plans.

▶CHAPTER AT A GLANCE
1. Poor prioritizers:
    Injudicious Jane—too easily influenced.
    Flighty Florence—too easily distracted.
    Insecure Ida—too afraid to act.
    Helpful Hannah—too busy to plan.
2. Christians can be assertive.
3. Good decision making is based on absolutes.
4. Learn to say no.
5. Be a smart prioritizer.

PART TWO: TAKE ACTION

FIVE
Eliminating Dinnertime Stress

Dinnertime is one of my favorite times of day. This isn't simply because I love to eat—although I do love to eat. I'm one of those people who can be inspired and even humored by the basic variety of fruits and vegetables. Would you have had the genius to invent the tiny blackberry or the cherry tomato? What about the huge, red watermelon or the odd-shaped squash? Compare that with the straight, light-green celery; the pointed, orange carrot; or the dark-green spinach leaf. This large variety shows that food was created for our enjoyment.

Besides, mealtime is more than merely eating. You have to eat alone for only a little while to know that mealtime is also a social event. Now that I work full time outside of the home, I know better than ever that dinnertime can be one of the most enjoyable times of day because it refreshes the body and reunites the family after a day full of activity. But preparing dinner can become a hassle. Why? For one thing, repetition can become monotonous. Think about how many dinners a woman will probably fix in an average lifetime. In approximately fifty years, she will cook some 18,250 dinners!

Second, if you are extremely busy, you know how easy it is to allow fatigue and lack of planning to get the best of your dinnertime cooking. The first few weeks after I began working were almost disastrous when it came to meal preparation. Like so many other women, I was racing down the supermarket aisles at about five o'clock in the evening to find something to eat. This almost eliminated my family's time together.

THE 30-DAY MENU SYSTEM

If you would just like to make the job of dinnertime cooking easier, here are some steps that can eliminate all the hassles that tend to make dinnertime a headache. The 30-Day Menu System goes beyond the traditional preparation of a regular menu to systematize all the steps that precede the actual meal preparation.

Every woman knows that getting the food on the table is only the last step in a long process. This process begins with deciding what to cook and making a menu. Next comes looking through cupboards to determine what ingredients you need to buy, writing shopping lists, clipping and sorting coupons (if you are a budget shopper), going shopping, and finally preparing the meal itself.

Then if you add a tired cook; hungry, whining children; a missing ingredient to the recipe that is already half prepared; an unplanned shopping trip; plus the knowledge that your family's health is depending on you; you have a process that is more complicated than it first appears. To use the 30-Day Menu System, first gather some favorite recipes, recipe cards, your monthly calendar, and shopping lists. Here is how the system works.

Pick a chef. The chef does not necessarily have to be you. Just about the time I began looking for help at our dinner hour, my eleven-year-old daughter, Kristine, was looking for some extra spending money. She was also anxious to learn to cook. Although it took extra work at the beginning to train my novice chef, the results have been better than I ever expected.

At first, she began the meals and I finished them when I arrived home. Three years later, she was still anxious to cook, and the pay of fifty cents a day made her feel like she had a part-time job. The satisfaction of really learning to cook also helped her remain interested. But best of all, I didn't have to cook on weekdays after coming home from work. It is important to establish who will be cooking on a given day so that you can select the right menu for the chef. A child helper needs a simple menu with an easy set of instructions. If family members are taking turns, the schedule should be posted so that each person knows when his turn comes up. Otherwise, some evening you might end up without any dinner!

Draw up the menu chart. Make a numbered list of
your thirty favorite menus (for example, see
appendix). Keep them simple yet nutritious. The
meals should be basic favorites with desserts such as
fruit or pudding. Thirty menus lend a surprising
amount of variety. And if you use these menus only on
working days, it takes about six weeks to use every
menu on the chart.

The 30-Day Menu Chart provides plenty of
flexibility as well. You do not have to use the menus
in consecutive order. If you like to eat quiche more
than once each month, put down its number as often
as you like. You can schedule your menus to take
advantage of grocery sales. Our menu chart was
additionally flexible because, as Kristine's cooking
skills improved, I substituted more challenging menus
for her to use.

Organize your menu chart so that all of the
hamburger meals are grouped together, the ham dishes
in another section, and so on. This way, you don't have
to hunt all over the chart to find the menu you're
looking for. The last ten meals are especially quick
meals. They are designed for those busy times when
food has to compete with after-school activities and
evening classes.

Since my menu is designed to keep things simple, I
have only two dinners that require some preparation
the prior evening. These are marked with an asterisk
beside the menu number. When *3 is posted for
tomorrow's dinner, I know that I need to begin my

beef broth the evening before for the next day's beef soup. If a week is going to be particularly hectic, I don't put either of these meals on the calendar.

Make a shopping chart. The 30-Day Shopping Chart eliminates wasting time to re-decide what each meal needs as you make out a weekly shopping list. The shopping chart helps take some of the repetition and tedium out of preparing dinner. It coincides with the menu chart, so that if you decide to have menu numbers 1, 15, 10, *3, and 18 this week, you simply look under these same numbers on the shopping chart to know exactly what ingredients you need for those meals (see chart B).

Making up this shopping chart does take some time initially. You have to look up the recipes in your cookbook or card file and write down all the necessary ingredients. But once that is done, you will never need to do it for that meal again.

Prepare matching recipe cards. The 30-Day Recipe Cards (see chart C) are responsible for the good job of cooking that Kristine has done. She has all the instructions she needs to complete these recipes. At first, a child doesn't know what menu item takes the longest time to cook, so to coordinate the meal the recipes are written in step-by-step order. At the top right-hand corner of every recipe card I put a total preparation time to help the cook have dinner on the table at the appropriate time. In each recipe I also remind the cook to cover and chill fresh fruits and vegetables until dinner to avoid losing valuable vitamins.

The thirty recipes I use require a combination of scratch and packaged ingredients. For instance, scalloped potatoes take too long if they are homemade but are still tasty from a box. Since we like to eat dinner at a reasonably early hour, the recipe cards are made with a time limit in mind. These recipe cards will save you the time each day that you would spend in instructing a beginning chef.

Post your monthly calendar. On this calendar, you write the recipe number for each working day during the present week. The chef then knows to pull out her recipe card with the same number, and has complete instructions needed to serve that meal.

Organize a shopping trip. When making your shopping list, look up the menu numbers that you have posted on your calendar and correlate them with your shopping chart (see chart B). Look to see which ingredients you have in the cupboards and list every item you will need to buy on your next shopping trip. Organize the list, shop, and then enjoy not making any unplanned trips to the supermarket.

Following is a description of one week's system. First the menus for each day were chosen and posted (chart A). Then the shopping list for the items needed was made out (chart B). Finally the recipe card for each day (chart C) was pulled out of the file and followed for a delicious, well-balanced dinner—on time and hassle free! (For a copy of my complete 30-Day Menu Chart, see the appendix.)

CHART A

A SAMPLE WEEK

Monday	Tuesday	Wednesday	Thursday	Friday
11	12	13	14	15

THE 30-DAY MENU CHART (a five-day sample)

1 Simple Quiche
     Toast
     Fruit cup

15 Baked ham and pineapple
      Biscuits
      Peas
      Carrot sticks
      Pudding

10 Swedish meatballs
      Brown rice
      Peas and carrots
      Sliced apples

*3 Beef vegetable soup
      Crackers
      Oatmeal cake

18 Fish fillets
      Scalloped potatoes
      Cooked cabbage
      Fruit cup

CHART B

THE 30-DAY SHOPPING CHART (a five-day sample)

1	frozen deep pie shell, margarine, flour, milk, eggs, salt, pepper, green onions, cheese, bacon, bread, 2 each: apples, oranges, bananas
15	7 individual ham slices, 1 can pineapple rings, cloves, biscuit mix or makings, frozen peas, fresh carrots, pudding mix
10	1½ pounds ground beef, 2 envelopes dry onion soup mix, brown rice, salt, frozen peas and carrots, 4 apples
*3	1 pound beef stew meat, beef soup starter mix, crackers, quick oatmeal, shortening, sugar, brown sugar, eggs, vanilla, flour, wheat germ, baking soda, salt, nutmeg, butter, cream or milk, coconut, nuts
18	6 fish fillets, 2 packages scalloped potatoes, cabbage, salt, pepper, 1 can fruit cocktail, 2 bananas

CHART C

THE 30-DAY RECIPE CARDS (a five-day sample)

1

Simple Quiche, toast, fruit cup

Prep time:
1 hour, 10 minutes

Quiche: Preheat oven to 375°. In a saucepan, melt 4 Tbsp margarine. Stir in ¼ cup flour. Add 1 cup warm milk. Quickly stir in 4 beaten egg yolks, ½ tsp salt, dash pepper. Beat egg whites till stiff and fold into egg-yolk mixture. Into frozen pie shell put 1½ cups grated cheese, 4 strips cooked bacon, and 2 chopped green onions with tops. Pour on egg mixture. Bake 35-40 minutes or until set. Let stand 10 minutes before serving.
Fruit cup: When quiche has baked for 30 minutes, cut up 2 each: apples, oranges, and bananas. Put in bowl, cover, and chill until dinner. *Toast:* At last minute toast bread.

15

Baked ham and pineapple, biscuits, peas, carrot sticks, pudding

Prep time:
45 minutes

Ham: Arrange 7 ham slices in baking dish. Top with 1 can sliced pineapple and ½ can pineapple juice. Sprinkle with whole cloves. Bake at 350° for 30 minutes.
Biscuits: While ham is baking, make biscuits according to package directions or recipe; bake during the last 10 minutes of the ham baking time.
Peas: Cook frozen peas according to package directions.
Carrots: Slice carrot sticks and cover.
Pudding: Mix pudding according to package directions; refrigerate until dessert.

10

Swedish meatballs, brown rice, peas and carrots, sliced apples

Prep time:
55 minutes

Rice: Put 5 cups water and 2 tsp salt in a 3-quart saucepan; bring to a boil. Add 2 cups rice and stir once. Cover and simmer on low heat for 45 minutes.
Meatballs: Combine 1½ pounds ground beef and 1 envelope dry onion soup mix in a bowl. Mix well and shape into 1½ inch balls. Brown in skillet on all sides. Add 1 more package dry onion soup mix with 2½ cups water to meatballs. Simmer covered on low heat for 20 minutes.
Peas and carrots: Cook peas and carrots according to package directions. *Apples:* Slice 4 apples, cover, and refrigerate.

*3   *Prep time:*
Beef vegetable soup, crackers, oatmeal cake   1½ hours

Beef vegetable soup: Add beef soup starter mix to beef stock,
including stew meat, prepared the night before; simmer
90 minutes.
Oatmeal cake: Combine 1 cup quick oatmeal, 1½ cups boiling
water, ½ cup shortening, ½ cup sugar, ½ cup brown sugar,
2 eggs, 1 tsp vanilla, 1 cup flour, ⅓ cup wheat germ,
1 tsp baking soda, ½ tsp salt, dash nutmeg. Stir well.
Pour batter into a greased and floured 9x9 pan. Bake at 350°
for 25 minutes.
Frosting: Mix together 6 Tbsp melted butter,
⅔ cup brown sugar, ¼ cup cream or milk, 1 cup coconut,
¾ cup chopped nuts. When cake is done baking, spread over
top of cake and bake 10 minutes more.
At the last minute, put crackers on the table.

---

18   *Prep time:*
Fish fillets, scalloped potatoes, cooked cabbage, fruit cup 45 minutes

Scalloped potatoes: Prepare potatoes according to box
directions. Bake 45 minutes at 350°.
Fish fillets: When potatoes have baked for 15 minutes, put fish
into baking dish in oven. Bake for 30 minutes or until fork tender.
Cabbage: Cut whole cabbage into small pieces. Put in large
saucepan with 1 cup water. Cover and simmer on low for
30 minutes or until fork will go through cabbage easily.
Add salt and pepper.
Fruit cup: Mix 1 can fruit cocktail with 2 bananas. Cover and
chill until dinner.

Solving the dinnertime hassles takes an initial time
investment. However, the time and frustration you save
will be worth it.

The other night upon returning home from work, I walked from the garage into the family room and the smells from the kitchen were a welcomed greeting. As I said hello to each of the children and listened to their news of the day, I noticed the burning candle on the mantel. I was glad to be home. I knew that whether we decided to eat in front of the TV, on the back porch, or at the dining-room table, our dinnertime together would be the relaxing time it should be.

▶CHAPTER AT A GLANCE
1. Pick a chef.
2. Draw up the menu chart.
3. Make a shopping chart.
4. Prepare matching recipe cards.
5. Post your monthly calendar.
6. Organize a shopping trip.

SIX
Managing the Children

Taking the hassle out of homemaking has as much to do with managing people as with managing things. If you have children, you already know that raising them takes some real imagination and good, old-fashioned work.

Child hassles can get the best of any mother. When a child leaves toys everywhere, gets into things he shouldn't, or decides to do his own will instead of yours, it doesn't exactly brighten your day. Or how about when he neglects his chores, uses too much shampoo, stays out too late, neglects proper eating habits, or is just too noisy? Children have a way of requiring our best home-management skills, to say the least.

Keeping child hassles at their minimum requires the same steps in planning that you would use for any other hassle. The difference is that you continually modify the plan as the child grows and changes. This is an area in which the home manager cannot be passive—she must get actively involved. The active home manager does invest time initiating plans, but later she saves countless hours she might have spent solving problems. Why not spend time giving them positive direction rather than trying to repair negative behavior?

POSITIVE STEPS TOWARD ELIMINATING HASSLES

Now that our children are all in their teens, I am convinced four actions are essential to managing children with the least amount of hassles.

Channel your kids' creative energy in positive directions. At times a healthy child's energy and enthusiasm seem to have no limits. That is why children can be so much fun or so much of a hassle. The stress of an adult's life often stifles this creative energy that is so abundant in a child. I have found that one of the best ways to channel our kids' creative energy is by teaching them the value of working with their hands to make crafts or to decorate the home. Crafts can be introduced to even small children by using clay, crayons, glue, beads, paints—almost anything that keeps their little hands busy.

Older children require craft projects with a little more imagination. However, we have spent two very nice evenings coloring in the beautiful adult coloring books available. I enjoy it myself; it is very relaxing. If you enjoy making things but you can't think of what you would like to do, your local craft store probably has a wonderful selection of craft ideas.

I am keeping my eyes open continually for the perfect craft or decorating idea to introduce to my three teenagers, who always seem to have some excess energy to apply to new ideas. Even if only one child picks up on an idea I introduce, and enjoys it, I consider it a success. Everyone needs to experience the feeling of accomplishment that comes from creating something. I have often felt stress leave my body when I sat down to work on a craft. To be happy, we all need to express our creativity.

A new craft idea caused some enthusiasm at our house last summer. It is the answer for anyone who really enjoys art but can't draw particularly well. It is called stencil art, that wonderful, easy way of decorating walls, wood, fabric, or metal. You simply tape the stencil onto the object you want to decorate and brush on the paint. When you lift the stencil, you leave a perfect design.

The children put ducks and flowers (with my assistance) on the kitchen walls and pantry doors. It was so much fun arranging a scene on each wall by using our imaginations. One wall has a structured flower scene. Another has flowers placed in an almost random pattern. How creative we felt! We also stenciled festive bags to use for gift wrapping at Christmas. Then Mindy, our oldest daughter, stenciled teddy bears and flowers on her bedroom walls. Her whole room became an adorable den of bears filled with matching embroidery-hoop bears, bear pictures, bear puzzles hung on the wall, and stuffed bears seated on a child's school chair and rocking chair. She even refinished the chairs herself. Her decorating filled her summer days and fulfilled her need to create.

Besides craft ideas, I try to find other activities that are fun. One year my mother came up with just such an activity as a Christmas gift for our three kids when they were in grade school. She mailed each child a notebook with instructions. Each child was to write, color, paste pictures, or draw in these books until the books were completely full. Then they were to mail them back to Grandma. These books were definitely original creations and they filled many evenings that otherwise could have been boring. Grandma also has some dear treasures of their young years.

You can create fun activities at the spur of the moment or by careful planning. They can be little silly things or grand things. They need not occur too often—just when you feel your children need something fun to do. One simple activity that is easy and inexpensive is to have a special dinner. These dinners can be eaten by candlelight with an out-of-the-ordinary menu. A special dinner can celebrate anything: the end of the school year, the start of a new year, a new job, a special achievement.

One of the most successful celebrations we ever had was some years ago when everything in our family seemed to be going wrong. My husband couldn't find work, and it looked as though we were going to go under financially. Our morale needed a boost. So the children and I planned a big "thanksgiving" dinner to celebrate. At that time, I couldn't think of many positive things in our lives to celebrate, other than the fact that we were Christians. So we celebrated just that—the fact that we were Christians. That day our morale rose to a new high, and we had the greatest, happiest day we had experienced for a long time. To add icing to the cake, my husband got a fine job offer the next morning.

Another avenue for channeling young energy is through educational activities. Red Cross classes, baby-sitting workshops, park district and recreation classes, science centers, and cultural centers are a few good possibilities. Finding what will interest your child, especially if he is a teenager, takes some thinking on your part. You have to look at his or her talents, interests, and abilities. Actually, you need to keep your eyes and ears open for any possible ideas or clues that let you know what your child may find interesting.

Create a positive environment in your home.
This is important when it comes to keeping hassles at a minimum. Creating a positive climate can be difficult or easy; it all depends on the woman home manager. Children are much like adults. When we feel understood, loved, esteemed, and supported, our outlook will probably be positive. When we feel misunderstood, ridiculed, or shoved aside, we react accordingly. Our environment can either help us or hinder us from maintaining a positive attitude.

A positive environment is impossible without communication among family members. Statistics show that poor communication is one of the major causes of family problems. Whenever you think of trying to promote open sharing in any group, you usually think of talking. But Carl Rogers, a communications expert, says, "Man's inability to communicate is a result of his failure to listen effectively, skillfully, and with understanding to another person."

Listening to your children can solve a host of potential hassles. If we understand our children, we won't be spectators who have to guess what is going on in their lives. Spectating in a relationship is dangerous, because if you don't know the thoughts of another person, you can easily misunderstand his actions. Some people only try to guess what the other person's motives are instead of carefully listening to him. Too easily, accusations and further problems escalate simply because there is no sharing between family members. They are spectators rather than participants.

When my three children were in grade school, I recognized that I had a real problem listening to them. One night I took a good look at my inability to listen. I really did want to be a good mother. But when the kids were small, I hadn't had this kind of trouble relating to them. Suddenly they were older, and I wasn't making the transition very well. Why was it so hard for me? Maybe it was because I had to invest more time. I couldn't put the kids to bed as early and pursue my personal activities. I had to begin knowing the children as people with their own opinions and problems. I knew I might have to give up some of the things I wanted to do. "Dear God," I prayed, "you are a God of miracles, and if you can make me a mother who listens to her family, you will have done a real miracle in my life."

I came to understand that the person to whom my child talked would be the person who would have the greatest influence on him. The way things were going, I knew it wouldn't be me. And, if it wasn't me, I had no guarantee what counsel my three children would receive. So, I reached for pen and paper. I asked myself how long I thought it would take me to work this thing out. I wrote down one year. I then wrote down three pointers I felt would help me reach my goal to become a listening parent.

The first thing I wrote was to *sit down*. I pride myself in being able to do more than one thing at a time, like talk on the phone while I scrub the kitchen floor. But if I was going to become a good listener, I would have to break this old habit. I was always doing something else while the kids were talking. It was like pulling teeth for me to stop in the middle of a project just to sit—just to sit and listen to a child's concerns. I'd much rather think about my own concerns anyway. But I learned.

When I could see that a child was calling for my undivided attention, I did force myself to sit down and concentrate on what was being said. As I began to hear the words they spoke, I began to see three children living in my house whom I didn't know very well. I tried to look beyond the childish prattle to both see and know my own child. Much to my pleasure, I found that if I sat and listened today it would save endless chatter tomorrow that might be coming from a child talking merely to gain attention. Also, I found that the children wanted only to share the news of the day and then run off to play.

The second pointer I wrote was to *be quiet*. Frankly, there is nobody that I would rather listen to than myself. When I am talking, I am really interested. But, if I have to listen to the problems of a child, I like to pinpoint the problem quickly and give three easy steps toward solving it. The only trouble is that we never seem to get to the real problem that way. My magnificent answers are to questions that aren't even being raised.

A wise proverb was written for people like me. It says, "He who gives an answer before he hears, it is folly and a shame to him" (Prov. 18:13, NASB). I was going to have to close my mouth if I wanted to hear what was really being said.

I learned my first lesson when my daughter Mindy was obviously frustrated for several days. When I asked her what the problem was, her answer was simple: "I hate school."

"What is it about school that you don't like?"

"Everything." She tossed her long brown hair over her shoulder for emphasis. Normally, her eyes were bright with enthusiasm, but now they studied the floor. I knew I needed to inquire further.

"How long have you felt this way?" I asked.

"I've always hated school."

"Now, let's see. Do you like recess?" When she answered yes, I went on down the list until I found a likely stopping place. She then described a particular girl with whom she was having trouble. I was delighted to have finally found the real problem. But, by listening and rephrasing her answers back to her, I could see we still hadn't reached the thing that was bothering her the most.

Finally she said, "My teacher is grouchy; she doesn't like me at all."

An hour later, after many tears, she was able to identify what had been tormenting her for days. She had overheard a girl talking about her to the teacher. The girl was a habitual liar. So when the teacher was a little more grouchy than usual, she was sure the teacher had believed the girl. Now Mindy was a miserable fifth grader. She had convinced herself that she didn't like the teacher anyway and that it didn't matter to her. But it did matter, and she was a hassle to live with as a result.

After we had talked, she knew that she needed to talk to her teacher. Getting the problem out in the open and knowing I would be praying for her set her mind at ease. She hugged me and skipped off to bed.

The next day I called the teacher. I found out that the school was trying to get help for the troubled girl, who was even telling lies about the teacher all over school. The teacher was also able to volunteer some helpful information.

"You know, I've had a terrible cold and have been a little grouchy the last couple of weeks. Maybe Mindy took it personally. I'll talk to her today." I was glad I had taken time to hear this problem.

One of the hardest times to keep my mouth shut was when our son, Mark, was sharing a problem that had gotten the best of him. Generally, he was very practical and able to look ahead to a solution. This time he was fighting back the tears. He was obviously angry and hurt. Mark's dark-complected face, dark hair and eyes usually added to his huge smile and dimples. But now his glasses were misty from tears and he was speaking words I was afraid to hear. He used words like *hate* and said he never wanted to see his friend again.

I had made a little rule with myself that I wouldn't offer advice until the child made some indication that he was ready to hear. Usually, this happened when he was completely finished with what he had to say. This time, though, it was harder than usual to be quiet, for I could feel a sermon rising up within me; I wasn't sure I could trust Mark to do the right thing with these emotions.

But hadn't I previously said these words myself to the heavenly Father? I knew God needed to hear the whole truth before he could bring me to a better place. So I relaxed and listened to the vindictive feelings with no judgment.

When my son finished, he seemed to be looking for some comment from me. It was then that I had the chance to help him look at the situation more realistically and honestly.

"Son, I know you are hurt because you think you have lost your friend. You are angry at him for what he has done because you don't think he likes you anymore. Maybe you both can talk it over and work it out."

Later, he gave me a big hug and ran off to bed. I assured him that I would be praying about the situation. He was growing up, and I knew I would have to trust his wisdom in working this problem out his way. The next day he came running home from school with that big smile to let me in on the good news: he and his friend had made peace.

The third pointer, and for me the most important, is to *keep trying to listen.* So many things come up that distract me from my intention to be a listening mom. Two years after I embarked on my resolution, I had to go to work full time and so my time at home became even more valuable. But I knew I wasn't fighting my listening obligation quite as much, even though I was tired after a full day's work. Listening is still a commitment that I have to renew often.

Whenever I seem to lose contact with a child, I force myself to keep trying. A sense of losing contact may be a cue to have breakfast alone with the child to become reacquainted. It is not a cue to give up.

By listening to my children, I am finding that I have

a lot more patience with them because I know what is going on in their worlds. Also, I feel comfortable spending time alone or with my husband because I know the kids are not being neglected. Nowadays the whole family is spending more time enjoying things together because we have grown to know each other in a new way. Potential hassles are being "nipped in the bud," so we have more time to enjoy living together instead of going from one small problem to another.

I have wondered how the kids view my ability to listen to them. Though it has been a real struggle for me, I have hoped that they feel comfortable talking to me. My answer to this question came the other day as Mindy was telling me about a girl at school. "You know, Mom, Sheri says she never talks to her mom. Can you believe someone would not tell her mom the things she is going through?"

She was amazed at the prospect and I was glad. She knew she could talk to me.

Give your child clear, specific guidelines. This is the third thing I believe is very important in order to take the hassle out of child management. A child cannot succeed unless he knows what he is supposed to do. And he won't know how well he is doing unless you tell him. Household responsibility is a good way to provide success for your child. Every person wants to feel as if he is a meaningful contributor to the team effort. Every person wants to feel needed and appreciated. But how you go about creating such success depends largely on your having clear, specific guidelines.

Household responsibility can be assigned to each family member on his personal chore list. First write a list of things that need to be done, and then divide them equally among the family members. (For specific examples and charts for delegating responsibility, see my book *The Woman's Complete Home Organizer*, Tyndale House, 1984.)

Successful teamwork is about the best thing that can happen to any group of people, especially the people you live with day after day. But successful teamwork doesn't just happen; you make it happen. Getting the family involved in the day-in, day-out tasks to maintain the home takes a little work on your part. However, it will save you hours of work later and will add family respect if everyone does his share.

Whatever household assignments you give, make sure you go through the procedure with the child. He not only needs to know what to do but exactly how to do it. Do the task with each child twice—first you demonstrate and then have him do it. That way he will know what the job involves and how to succeed at it. At the beginning, check the work daily so you can be sure he is doing it. Later on, when he has mastered the task, keep your eyes open to check but don't let him think he needs supervision. Give the child a specific time frame for becoming proficient in the task (maybe one or two weeks). Proficient means doing the job without any reminders from you to get it done. At our house, I give each child a five o'clock deadline for all chores to be completed. Last of all, be specific about his success in mastering the job. Tell him exactly what he is doing right.

Besides household tasks, you must spell out other responsibilities in detail to assure that the child understands what is expected of him or her. For example, dating guidelines can't be left undefined. Help your child succeed by discussing these matters ahead of time and providing the necessary information and support.

Allow independence whenever you possibly can. As your child becomes older and more dependable, you should encourage independent thinking and action. An older child needs to be given certain projects that can be done his or her way with little adult supervision.

The Bible admonishes parents to train up a child in the way he should go, but that doesn't mean forcing the child to think only as we do. I believe that after a child is twelve years old, he is basically trained. By that age you must have a strong relationship with your child or you will probably have little ongoing influence. In some cultures a child is considered an adult at a much younger age than in the United States. I believe the responsibility must slowly shift from parent to child, and that it should happen before the child leaves home. That still leaves some time for you to gently guide the child if it is needed.

We must be careful to teach our children to be responsible instead of irresponsible. Let's say your child wants to make a decision and you don't know if he is yet able to handle the situation completely. Since it probably isn't a life or death situation, you have two choices: you can make the decision for him or you can discuss it with the child and allow him to try out the situation and get back to you for further discussion. If you always insist on making the decisions, especially for an older child, you may somewhat succeed at modifying his behavior, but you probably won't change how he feels about it. Let's face it. If someone insists you adopt his opinion, you will probably feel annoyed even if you agree with him.

Allowing children to become responsible for their own actions requires the woman home manager to respect and value opinions other than her own. My children like things I don't like and they have other opinions than I do, and I'm glad. They add to my life that way. Variety is healthy; we can all learn from each other. Some of the things I believe today came through time and experience. My children will have to live their lives as adults the way they see best, and learn from their own experiences.

As a child becomes more independent, the real issue is not that he does everything perfectly. Some of his decisions will have to be wrong just as some of your decisions were wrong. The point is that decision making is necessary in order to become responsible, successful adults, and that takes practice.

A weekly or monthly allowance is one important way of fostering healthy independence. Each child in the house needs some money for projects, movies, and parties. This money needs to be under his own control. I don't like to make it a payment for chores because one team member doesn't pay another for being a part of the team. Each child at our house gets twenty dollars a month. I do pay them additional money for chores they volunteer to do above and beyond the call of duty. You may feel you can't afford to pay that kind of an allowance. But I find I spend that much or more when I give them money as the occasions arise.

Because our children have handled their own allowances for years, they have a better appreciation for money. They also have become hardworking people who are able to earn extra money by baby-sitting, doing yard work, and other odd jobs.

Trust is involved in allowing a child to become more independent. Since the child communicates with you, and you understand how he thinks, you know how much responsibility he can handle. I guess I shall never understand why some mothers demand that their children ask for permission before they make any move at all. If the same mother were keeping a close watch, she would know how much responsibility the child could handle.

I encourage our three teenagers to make decisions as they need to. I simply want to know what they decide. If they go somewhere and I'm not home for them to ask, I want a note left on the refrigerator.

As you take the hassle out of child management, remember that your flexibility is essential. Be open to change because your child is changing. If you need some advice about a specific hassle in your home, you may find that the child himself could have the best solution for the problem. Ask him what he would do.

▶CHAPTER AT A GLANCE

1. Channel your kids' creative energy in positive directions.
2. Create a positive environment in your home.
3. Give your child clear, specific guidelines.
4. Allow independence whenever you possibly can.

SEVEN
Housekeeping without Headaches

Housework is an experience shared by all. Everyone knows about the necessity to keep house, but few people really enjoy housework. It is a repetitious job: you wash the dishes just to get them dirty again—three or four times each day. You fold the nice, fluffy, clean towels, put them on the shelf, and before you know it, those same towels lie in a wet heap on the bathroom floor. How about the bed you make? Just hours later the blankets resemble a troubled sea. And so it goes—over and over again.

Just because housework is repetitious does not mean it is easy. Keeping the house involves a long list of duties. See if reading this list doesn't make you tired!

Making beds
Planning and cooking meals
Packing lunches
Feeding animals
Vacuuming
Doing dishes
Straightening the house
Changing the sheets
Doing the laundry
Mopping floors
Sweeping porches

Dusting the furniture
Cleaning the bathrooms
Ironing
Taking out the garbage
Mending clothes
Folding the laundry
Cleaning closets and cupboards
Washing windows
Cleaning kitchen appliances
Taking care of the outside grounds

This list is exhausting, but not exhaustive. It only illustrates the numerous duties that come under the heading of housework.

The personalities of the women who keep house are as varied as the duties they perform. Have you noticed that some women keep perfect closets while the rest of the house is unkempt? Other women keep an orderly house but the closets look like disaster areas. Some homemakers clean weekly. Others clean spontaneously when they get in the mood. And some homemakers clean a little at a time so that they never have a cleaning day per se.

Whatever kind of homemaker you are, you know that no matter how mundane housework may seem, it still has intrinsic value. Most people feel more content when the house is neat. Besides, it is a lot easier trying to find something if it is in its proper place. It is easier to fix a sandwich if there is a clean plate to put it on. In addition, housework says some things to the people with whom you live. When the house looks nice, your family feels proud to display it to friends and to neighbors. Thus, a clean, orderly home enhances family pride. I have noticed that this pride is present even in young children.

Housework is important for another reason: it teaches children (without a sermon) the value of responsibility. Children learn by what they see. They don't learn if we talk about the importance of housework but don't follow our talk with action. If we home managers let things slide, children feel comfortable about letting their own areas of responsibility slide.

Housekeeping has still another important function in that it sets a secure, peaceful atmosphere if things are in order. The people in the house find it easier to relax. A home that is orderly lets the family know that someone is in charge. The family feels more secure than it would feel if everything were chaotic. So housework, mundane as it seems, is a means toward achieving important goals in our family life: family harmony, family security, responsible children, children who respect parents' leadership.

FIXED AND VARIABLE ESSENTIALS

How clean is clean, and how orderly should a house be? Of course, each homemaker must determine this herself. Each woman must find her own comfort level.

I divide my tasks into two categories and treat each group differently. The first group I call *fixed essentials* in that they are tasks that I cannot let go without disrupting family peace. The second group I call *variable essentials* because they are tasks that must be done eventually, but not immediately.

Fixed essentials are mainly my daily duties. For instance, if I don't have dinner on the table, that is disrupting for five hungry people. Other things include doing laundry daily to keep ahead on clean clothes and towels; putting dirty dishes in the dishwasher so no dirty dishes are left in the sink; and house straightening so that there is never a buildup of debris.

The second group of tasks—variable essentials—can be done less often. The oven does need to be cleaned from time to time, but probably no one will notice if it were let go for a while. However, if you turn on the oven and it begins to smoke from lack of cleaning, that project would immediately become a fixed essential! Variable essentials cannot be neglected for long periods of time, but they are certainly more flexible.

After I went to work outside of the home full time, I found that I needed to extend the time between doing some of my variable-essential tasks. For instance, I began changing the sheets every two weeks instead of every week, and I staggered the different beds in the house so as not to wash all the sheets at once. I found that I could do this with many household tasks, and the family would in no way be disrupted.

However, after I went to work, the fixed-essential duties became more pressing. If I neglected to fold the towels in the evening, I would have no time to do it the next morning before work. The family would likely be showering without clean towels.

KEEPING MOTIVATED

Even though we know that housework is important, it is often hard to keep motivated. We want to do good jobs, and we believe we should, but motivation can disappear so easily. Without motivation, we are at a loss because motivation is what puts our beliefs into action.

Through the years, I have found four things that help me keep motivated in my homemaking tasks.

Work within your energy level. At times I have less energy than others and I want something to do that doesn't require mental concentration. Housework comes in handy then because I can work off stress and not have to use my mind in the process. I have found that if I am nervous or anxious about something, I can channel that nervous energy into productive work. Sometimes when I am finished with the cleaning, I have forgotten why I was nervous in the first place.

Since I don't do a lot of cooking at our house, I have found that spending the afternoon on Saturday in the kitchen does wonders for my mental health. Working with my hands relaxes my mind and body. I always feel better when I can see the product of my cleaning or baking. That refreshes me.

Use a five-minute motivator. I have talked about this five-minute motivator before, but it works in keeping house just as it does in other areas in which you lack motivation. Getting motivated is much harder if you have a big project you are dreading. However, if you decide to work for only five minutes, you will begin the dreaded task. And having begun, you often stick with it longer. Still, five-minute segments on any task will bring eventual completion. You would be surprised at the power of only five minutes of steady work.

Incorporate change as a motivator. Change stimulates us and motivates us. Cleaning the same house over and over again is no fun if it remains completely the same. Everyone needs a change now and then to brighten up the task. A gallon of paint does wonders for my approach to homemaking. I need to be fixing up the place a little at a time or I get bored with it. Often I will buy a new candle, a small bouquet of flowers, or a new poster. Anything that brightens my attitude is well worth the little amount of money I spend. The other family members will be much more anxious to pitch in if they see change from time to time.

There are also ways to create change without spending any money. How about rearranging the furniture or trying a new recipe? Lighting can enhance different pictures or centerpieces and thus create the illusion of change. Turning out the lights for a candlelight dinner, or moving the dinner outdoors, stimulates my homemaking efforts. I need it, and I believe my family needs it.

Convert your homemaking tasks into minutes.
This is somewhat of a mind game I play with myself, but it works. I used to think about the tasks I had to do; now I think about the time I am going to spend.

I simply estimate the amount of time I need to vacuum and I tell myself that I am going to spend ten minutes vacuuming the living room and dining room. I really don't mind investing ten minutes, even though I don't like vacuuming. If I tell myself that I must move the furniture, drag out the vacuum, and then vacuum two whole rooms, it sounds like too much work. Sometimes I give myself just three minutes in the bathroom, and you would be surprised how much can get done in such a small amount of time. I feel comfortable not doing the entire bathroom at once because I can always invest three more minutes the next day.

On the next page is an actual timed list of some typical household duties done at a normal pace to illustrate how changing tasks into minutes makes them seem easier.

These items illustrate that most homemaking chores don't take much time if a woman works nonstop. Changing tasks into minutes is how I keep from spending too much time all at once. In other words, if I tell myself that I am willing to invest twenty minutes each day in actual housecleaning, I find I never have to have cleaning day on the weekends when I am off

35 seconds	Clean bathroom sink (liquid cleanser)
5 minutes 30 seconds	Vacuum living/dining rooms (moving only small furniture)
90 seconds	Clean two bathroom mirrors and hall mirror
5 minutes 40 seconds	Clean kitchen after making waffles
35 seconds	Empty garbage
70 seconds	Fold ten towels

work. Also, I can do a little cleaning here and there without getting tired of it.

Get the family involved. When we talk about housework we must talk about teamwork. Each family member should be carrying his share of the load. Since every family member shares the benefits of a smooth-running home, each member should share the responsibility. Creating a team effort is invaluable. When even the children in the house feel good about their contribution to the overall team effort, you have accomplished a great deal. You are not only getting the work done, but you are teaching some valuable lessons such as how to work together, how to support the team, and how to carry responsibility in the most important area of all: daily living.

Delegating household tasks is discussed in my book *The Woman's Complete Home Organizer,* so I will not go into it in detail. However, getting the family involved in homemaking is a consistent, long-term task. First, make a list of everything that needs to be done and when it needs to be done. Then distribute the tasks among the family members by using a weekly chore list. Write under each day of the week what each child must do for that particular day. Then train and hold each member accountable for his or her responsibility. Delegate simple chores to the very young child and adapt the chores as he grows, giving him responsibility according to his ability.

In our family, we allow our children to suffer the consequences of chores they neglect if the neglect persists for two or three days. Sometimes I add a new task on top of their daily task or turn off the TV for the evening. Now that the children are older and their activities take them out more often, we do most of our work on the weekends and do only our fixed essentials during the week.

I believe that children need to be taught at an early age that working is healthy and that we gain satisfaction from a job well done. I made chores a game when our children were young, and I rewarded a job well done with a word of praise or even a small purchased token. I would even sneak into their room and do a chore for them if I felt like they needed a lesson on the value of being part of a team that helps one another. For years, the three children would sneak into the room of a family member who was having a birthday and make his bed for a surprise.

My philosophy about teamwork is so strong that I

never delegate all of the responsibility to the kids, even if I would like to relax myself. I believe that even though I have worked all day, they too have worked in school and on homework. We all must carry our share. I have also taught the value of trading jobs so that when someone is more busy than normal, he can take a break from housework.

Eliminate troublesome areas. One way of lessening the work is by eliminating troublesome areas. I once had a hassle with a swivel chair because whoever sat in it would spin and make fingerprints and footprints on the wall next to it. No matter how often I pulled it out from the wall, that chair was still too close. First, I thought about painting the wall brown (I did that once in another house we lived in), and then I decided to get rid of the chair the first time I could find a good excuse. I will never have another swivel chair again.

I also try to eliminate troublesome tasks by using simple methods, such as buying comforters for all the beds so that beds are easy to make. If there are some wrinkles underneath, no one ever knows. I hope to get kitchen carpet because mopping and waxing floors is a hassle for me. I also plan to install an attractive wooden rail between the entryway and the living room to keep the dogs out of the living/dining area. If a troublesome area makes homemaking harder, not easier, it is time to think about getting rid of it altogether.

Establish a daily routine. A routine is something you do that you don't need to think about or plan. It's a pattern of activities like taking a shower and getting dressed each morning. My routine is so fixed that it would be hard to not do it. My fixed-essential household tasks are done daily and at about the same time. After I arrive home from work each day and have greeted the kids, I start a load of laundry. That way, the clothes will be dry before I go to bed, and I can sort them into stacks for each family member to fold. After I start the laundry, I check the dishwasher to see if it needs emptying before dinner. When I'm upstairs to wash up for dinner, I may swish out the bathroom sink with a liquid cleanser and do any necessary straightening. I complete my daily routine before I sit down to relax for the evening because once I sit down, I may not get up again.

Routines are a normal, healthy part of life and can save thinking, planning, and work. If a person does the daily routine, there will be no work buildup that requires a great amount of time later on. Establish a daily routine, and do it.

Housework need not be a hassle if everyone in the family is involved and you are working within your energy level and using change to keep you motivated. The pluses far outweigh the minuses if your work is done a little at a time using a daily routine. If a certain area is a real hassle, you may find you can eliminate part or all of it, delegate the responsibility, or invest five minutes daily until it is done.

➡CHAPTER AT A GLANCE

1. Determine your fixed and variable essentials.
2. Work within your energy level.
3. Use a five-minute motivator.
4. Incorporate change as a motivator.
5. Get the family involved.
6. Eliminate troublesome areas.
7. Establish a daily routine.

EIGHT
Organizing Purchases

Are you a wise shopper? Do you compare prices and try to get the best deal for your money? Most people don't want to pay more for an item than absolutely necessary. We all like a bargain. But have you thought about the fact that you can lose money on an item after you buy it? You could spend hundreds of unnecessary dollars.

My beautician told me last week that she and her husband have taken their TV in for the same repair twice in the last six months. The repairman told her that he would fix it at no charge the second time if she would present the receipt when she came to pick up the television. "We usually keep our repair receipts, but now we can't find the one we need. We may have to pay an additional eighty dollars," she moaned.

Another friend knows she lost money on her car by not requiring that the dealer honor the warranty. "It was the strangest thing. Every time I washed my new car, I noticed the paint was chipping more and more. I was very dissatisfied with the paint job from the beginning, but I didn't think they would repaint the car, so I didn't even talk to the dealer about it." The car is only four years old, but she is already getting estimates for a new paint job at her own expense!

Keeping track of your household purchases is not easy. Do you remember when—the year, the month—you bought your refrigerator or your washer and dryer? Do you know what kind of warranty they each had? What did the warranty cover and for how long? If some kind of free service was offered because you bought an extra service contract, did you take advantage of it? This information is important even for smaller items.

Often when you buy an item, the dealer will offer certain incentives to get you to purchase from his company. Last fall we bought a set of new tires for our car. The company that sold us the tires offered to rotate and balance our tires every five thousand miles free of charge. That service normally costs twenty-seven dollars. Each time we take advantage of the offer, we save twenty-seven dollars. Not only do we save the money, but we also extend the life of the tires because they wear more evenly.

KNOW YOUR WARRANTY RIGHTS

Many products are sold on the basis that the warranty given with the product is so good that the customer cannot lose. But the two-year warranty on used cars, which turns out to be a 15 percent discount on parts and labor at a high-priced dealership, is no warranty at all. Or how about the lifetime guarantee that is offered, but the seller requires all maintenance to be done in their service department, which has inflated prices?

It is important to read and understand what the company or manufacturer offers when you buy a product. A warranty is a statement by the seller that the product has certain properties and if, after you have purchased an item, the product does not have such properties, the seller will fix it, refund the money, or replace it. Under a federal act, any article that costs more than fifteen dollars must either have a limited warranty or full warranty. A product must use the words *limited warranty* if the warranty does not meet these minimum standards set out by the warranty act:

1. The warrantor must provide for the correction of defects, malfunctions, or failure to conform with the written warranty within a reasonable time and without charge to the consumer.
2. The warrantor must not impose limitation on the time length of any implied warranty on the product.
3. The warrantor must not exclude or limit consequential damages for the breach of any implied or written warranty unless the exclusion conspicuously appears on the face of the warranty.
4. If the product contains a defect after a reasonable number of attempts by the warrantor to remedy the defects or malfunction

in the product, the warrantor must permit you to elect either a refund or a replacement.

5. The only duty of the buyer as a condition of securing remedies is that of notification of the defect or of non-conformity to the written warranty.

Shop at reputable stores. You should never feel uncomfortable about taking an item back to the store from which you purchased it if you find that it does not meet quality standards. If you pay for an item, you should expect quality. Shopping at reputable stores that stand behind their products pays off. I shall never forget the day my husband walked into a store to do some shopping. He mentioned to the salesman that the pants he was wearing were defective. He had had the pants for more than a year but the zipper was somewhat crooked. Believe it or not, the salesman suggested he make an exchange. My husband walked out of the clothing store wearing a new pair of pants. Needless to say, we do much of our shopping at this particular store because it stands behind its products.

If you want to exchange an item and the salesman is reluctant to do that or refund your money, ask to speak to the manager. I recently bought a pair of tennis shoes for my son, and after only two weeks the stitching had come loose. When I took the shoes back to the store (a large, reputable company), I was informed by the salesman that I could exchange the shoes but I couldn't get my money back. The store only offered this particular brand of tennis shoes and I felt that particular brand of shoe would not last. I asked to speak to the manager. The manager was willing to refund my money after I told him my situation and let him know that I had to have a shoe that would last.

Set up a tickler file. Most stores want you to present your receipt when you exchange purchases. If you also want the warranty honored, you need a receipt to prove the time of purchase. This requires some record keeping. A normal household has many items with warranties that expire at different times during the year. To keep track of everything, I developed a tickler file. This is a simple yet effective practice. You set up a card file for each month of the year. If in January you know that in three months you need to get service on your car, you put a reminder in the April file. Then in April, as you look through your file, you will be reminded to get the service done.

This card file is the easiest way to keep track of family household purchases. Every time you buy an item, put down the necessary information on a card. If certain maintenance is needed in six months, you put a tickler card under the month it is due. If the warranty expires at the end of the year, put the card one month before it ends so you can take advantage of any servicing that may be necessary.

To set up your tickler file, buy four-by-six-inch index cards, dividers with the months of the year, a card box in which to put them, a stapler or paper clips, and glue. Use a card for each purchase to record the pertinent information for future reference and staple the receipt to the back of the card. Many of your purchases will be registered and put under the month in which they were purchased. Some of your purchases will be registered there and also under the months when service needs to be done. The card will also have the warranty-expiration date on it so that as each service is done, the card can be put under the month in which the next service is due. Finally, the card is put under the month in which the warranty expires.

At the beginning of each month there should be another index card to register all the purchases you have made that month. Then when you are trying to locate a particular item, you can find it quickly. If you are registering an item of clothing, put the initials of the person for whom it was bought. Your index card for each month could look something like this:

PURCHASES THIS MONTH		
Item	Cost	Store Where Purchased
1.		
2.		
3.		
4.		
5.		
6.		

The following pages may be photocopied and cut out to glue to the appropriate cards for recording individual purchases.

CLOTHING

Item:
Purchase date:
For whom:
Cost:
Store:
Special instructions:

SMALL APPLIANCE

Item:
Purchase date:
Cost:
Store:
Warranty exp. date:
Brand name:
Model no.:
Serial no.:
Special instructions:

MAJOR APPLIANCE

Item:
Purchase date:
Cost:
Store:
Service dates:
Warranty exp. date:
Brand name:
Model no.:
Serial no.:
Special instructions:

HOUSEHOLD EQUIPMENT

Item:
Purchase date:
Cost:
Store:
Warranty exp. date:
Brand name:
Model no.:
Serial no.:

HOUSEHOLD FURNISHINGS

Item:
Purchase date:
Cost:
Store:
Warranty exp. date:
Special instructions:

AUTO EQUIPMENT

Item:
Purchase date:
Cost:
Store:
Service dates:
Warranty exp. date:
Brand name:
Model no.:
Serial no.:

Here is an example of a registered purchase and a necessary tickler card used to jog your memory:

TICKLER CARD

Item: V.W. tires
Check odometer. Rotate tires
at 35,000 miles.

APRIL

AUTO EQUIPMENT

Item: V.W. Rabbit tires
Purchase date: Jan. 10, 1985
Cost: $310.00
Service dates: Rotate tires at 35,000 miles

JANUARY

Keeping track of your purchases will not only save you money, but will save you time. You will no longer need to rummage through a pile of unmarked receipts unable to find the one you are looking for. Be sure you train your children to record their own purchases. This will help them learn how to keep track of items they buy and will help you when you need to exchange the item. When they are old enough to do so, teach them how to exchange their own purchases.

Now, write on your calendar at the beginning of each month this statement: Check your tickler file. That will help you remember to check under the appropriate month to see what items may need a service call or what warranties are due to expire.

Write anything down that will help you keep track of
and maintain the things you buy.

▶CHAPTER AT A GLANCE

1. Know your warranty rights.
2. Shop at reputable stores.
3. Set up a tickler file.

NINE
Budgeting and Saving

Do these sentiments seem familiar to you?

—The more money I make, the less I have.

—My paycheck seems to take wings and fly away as soon as I get it.

—After the bills are paid, I don't have enough left over for the things I really want.

—Sometimes I wonder if I can even meet our monthly obligations.

At one time or another, almost everyone has financial difficulty. Even trained financial professionals can have money hassles. Here is a story about a woman who never took the time to apply to herself some of the principles she taught to others.

Sheila was an accountant for fifteen years. In the 1970s, she worked with the Chrysler Corporation helping car dealerships that were in financial trouble. Sometimes she aided small businesses in getting back on their feet financially. Other times she helped close down large dealerships that couldn't be salvaged.

One day Sheila found herself in financial trouble. She realized she had not come to grips with how she managed her own money. "I was concerned because I was a single parent and was forty thousand dollars in debt. I was working and spending money like crazy," Sheila told me.

It dawned on Sheila that if she were to lose her job, she didn't know how she would pay all of her bills. She also had to face an important fact about herself: she was addicted to credit buying. "When I got depressed, spending money made me feel better."

Sheila decided that she would have to break the spending habit; she would get out of debt and stay out. Because she was addicted to credit buying, she decided to operate strictly on a cash basis. This was one of the most difficult decisions she had ever made. Now, however, she is in control of her finances and has never felt better about herself.

USING CREDIT SAFELY

Credit buying isn't all bad if you are a safe borrower. Bernard Meltzer, one of America's most respected financial experts, cites several advantages of credit buying. But he recommends it only for those who are able to handle it. Here is Meltzer's Safe Borrowers Test as it appeared in his book *Bernard Meltzer Solves Your Money Problems:*

Problems:
1. When you dine out, do you leave a bigger tip when you use a credit card than when you pay cash?
2. Do you borrow to meet current bills?
3. Do you pass up an item because of its price when you pay cash, but buy the item when you can use a credit card?
4. Do you gamble with the money you borrow? (Remember, playing the stock market is gambling.)
5. Are you inclined to buy an expensive item you don't really need because of the easy-payment plan?
6. Do you use your charge accounts when you know you may not be able to meet the payments?
7. When you use your credit card, do you feel like a big shot?
8. Do you spend more than 20 percent of your after-tax income on debt repayment?
9. Are you more likely to buy something on impulse with a credit card than with cash?
10. Do you use your credit card to go on buying binges?

If you answer yes to any of the above questions, chances are you're not a safe borrower. Mr. Meltzer says that the more yes answers you have, the more unsafe a credit user you are.

Most debt counselors recommend the following policy: Take the figure for your monthly income after all of your deductions and spend no more than 15 percent of that amount on debt payments to stay out of trouble. Stop using credit cards right now if you are already paying on purchases you couldn't afford. Credit buying can be a real problem if you don't know how to handle it.

Still, Mr. Meltzer believes there are some credit-buying advantages for the person in control of his finances:

1. You can get the use of money for up to fifty-five days free of charge. Every credit card has a billing date; and you have twenty-five days from your billing date to make payment without interest being charged. If you make a purchase on your billing date, it won't appear on your bill until the next billing date, thirty days later. Thus, you have the use of free money for fifty-five days total. All the while, your money in the bank is picking up interest.

2. You can also take advantage of bargains. Let's say you are short of cash, and a store is selling a $500 TV for $350—a $150 savings. If you use your credit card and pay the TV off in six months, the interest will come to a little more than $15. You will still have saved $135.

3. You can avoid the pitfalls of the installment contract. Under an installment contract, the item is technically not yours until the very last payment is made. If you had only one payment to go and couldn't pay the rest, the item could be repossessed. Legally, you cannot sell such an item until it is paid for in full. But suppose you buy an item with your credit card. Once your card is accepted, the item is yours to do with as you wish with no threat of repossession.

4. You can get discounts with your credit card when you offer to pay cash. Companies that accept credit cards have to pay the credit card company or the bank 8 to 14 percent of the selling price. Often you can offer to pay cash if the store will discount the item 5 percent. Usually, they will agree and both of you will save money by you not using your card.

5. You can avoid the expense of traveler's checks. Most traveler's

checks cost about 1 to 2 percent of their value. Credit cards are free.

6. You can keep accurate records for tax purposes. With a credit card purchase, you get a receipt in addition to the monthly statement from the credit card issuer.

7. You have an excellent source of identification. Ask any traveler, and he'll tell you that you simply can't register in advance at a hotel without a credit card.

Money hassles are unlike any other kind of hassle because money influences so many areas of our lives. Money (or rather the lack of it) can limit your ability to decorate your home, buy the necessities of life, educate your kids, and have the recreational experiences that every person and family needs.

SETTING UP A BUDGET

Like every other hassle, money hassles can be brought under control to gain the financial freedom you want. Many experts agree on the following steps to help you gain control of your finances.

Assess your current income. Here is a chart to help you estimate your net yearly income:

Source of Income	Amount
Salaries and wages (net)	
Bonuses	
Commissions	
Tips	
Rental income	

Source of Income	Amount
Interest	
Dividends	
Pensions	
Other income	
Net yearly income	

Divide this total figure by twelve to establish your net monthly income.

Assess where your money goes each month.
Sheila feels this step cannot be overemphasized: Sit down and assess where your money is going—every penny for one month. She believes most of us aren't aware of how much we spend until we write it down. This is a necessary step before anyone can work up a realistic budget. Also total up your annual expenses such as income taxes, real estate taxes, social security, home owner's insurance and vacations. Divide this figure by twelve and include it in your monthly expenses.

Set up an estimated monthly budget. Use your spending assessment to determine the amount for each area. Your fixed expenses—regular payments for house, insurance, loans, and car—should be listed first. Your flexible living expenses—including utilities, gasoline, food, sundries, clothing, entertainment, and medical—should be listed second. Add up your projected expenses in each category and subtract that amount from your total net income.

Get out of debt by operating within your income. If your expenses are greater than your income, you are operating in debt. It is time to begin vigorously managing your spending habits. Here are two broad guidelines that will help you to operate soundly even if you are not in debt. First, cut back wherever you can. (A section of money-saving tips is included later in this chapter.)

Second, never buy on impulse. If impulse buying is a problem for you, don't go into a store unless you know ahead of time exactly what you are going to buy and exactly how much you are going to spend. Ask yourself these questions before you make any purchase: (1) Do I really need it? (2) Can I really afford it? (3) If I need it, have I researched the item so I will get the best product for the best price?

Establish an emergency fund. Saving for future emergencies is essential. None of us can be certain that we will not lose our jobs or become medically disabled. Every family should work toward saving enough money in an emergency fund to cover living expenses for at least six months in case the worst should happen. A good method for doing this, once you are out of debt, is to continue to pay the same amount of money that you used to spend on debt reduction into your emergency fund. When your emergency fund is sufficiently built up, you can put this monthly payment into savings.

Establish a savings plan. Besides your emergency
fund, a successful savings plan can do more to
improve your standard of living. Here are two
techniques to make saving easier: First, save for
specific goals. The family will be more enthusiastic
about saving money for a specific purpose. Set up
separate savings accounts for each major goal. Banks or
financial institutions won't limit you in the number of
accounts you can open. You may want a separate
account for medical expenses, for vacations, for home
improvement, or for education. Second, make your
money earn money. Most of us don't make our savings
work for us as hard as we work for our savings. Check
out various options for earning higher interest points
than in a regular savings account. Your local bank is
but one of many resources for finding out the many
ways to earn money from your savings.

Set financial goals. When you begin to set financial
goals, get the entire family involved in the process.
Children need to learn about money management
before they leave the nest. They need to know why
certain things need to wait while other things can be
purchased now. If they help decide the goals, they
will support the decisions.

What are the things you really want? List below ten
things you would like to have. List the amount of
money you need and when you want the items. Then
put a star by the one or two items that are the most
important to you right now.

Desires	Money Needed	Date Wanted
1.		
2.		
3.		
4.		
5.		
6.		
7.		
8.		
9.		
10.		

By openly listing your desires, you can begin to realistically coordinate your buying plans with your savings program.

MONEY-SAVING TIPS

Eat meals consisting of items in season.

Eat only as much meat as you need. A single portion need not be more than four ounces.

Stay away from prepared foods. Make your own TV dinners with leftovers, and put them in the freezer. Make your recipes from scratch instead of buying expensive mixes. Make more hot cereals instead of buying expensive cold cereals.

Buy in bulk quantities.

Take advantage of supermarket coupons and specials.

Use cold water washes.

Insulate your home when it needs it.

Shop during sales. Certain months are well known for sales. For instance, January is white-sale month. February is furniture-sale month. Garden supplies go on sale in August, refrigerators and washing machines in June and July.

Shop at garage sales.

Go to movies during economy hour.

Replace bulbs throughout the house with bulbs of lower wattage.

Do your own repairs as much as you can.

Maintain your home and equipment. This may cost you a little money now, but it will save you money in the long run. Properly oiling your lawn mower could make it last two more years. Bringing garden tools in out of the rain will make them last a lot longer. Painting your house before the paint peels off will avoid deterioration.

Have regular dental and health checkups. If you take care of your health and your teeth, you will save money in the long run.

Sew some of your own clothes.

Saving money is not easy. However, getting control of your money hassles will give you the freedom to do what you really want. It is often not more money we need, but more control to use what we have. Stewardship in this area can enhance freedom in many other areas of your life. You can experience the satisfaction of saving and investing, even on a moderate income.

▶CHAPTER AT A GLANCE

1. Use credit safely.

2. Set up an overall budget.

3. Assess your current income.

4. Assess where your money goes each month.

5. Set up an estimated monthly budget.

6. Get out of debt by operating within your income.

7. Establish an emergency fund.

8. Establish a savings plan.

9. Set financial goals.

TEN
Entertaining with Pleasure

Entertaining friends, neighbors, and relatives can be one of the most rewarding experiences we can have. It allows us the opportunity to interact with a wide variety of people, bring joy to ourselves and others, and have a lot of fun in the process.

I've always believed that entertaining could be a joy; yet for years I found entertaining more stressful than beneficial. You see, I was going about it the wrong way. I was trying too hard, spending more money than I could afford, and worrying so much about how the house looked that I would become exhausted when trying to entertain.

Still, I wanted to open my home to people and really enjoy doing so. I finally found a way to begin each entertaining experience without going into a nervous frenzy: I took a good look at how I felt and admitted my feelings. I began to accept the fact that I was not a natural entertainer and believed that I could learn to acquire the skill a little at a time. When I did those things, I was able to experience the true enjoyment of opening my home without the hassle.

STEPS TO ENJOYING ENTERTAINING

If you are like me, you will appreciate the following tips for the hassled entertainer. Even if you are a natural entertainer, you will enjoy some of the fun ideas I present later on in this chapter.

Decide on a no-fail menu. The first step for the hassled hostess is to use simplicity. For best results, don't try out new recipes on guests. Rather, follow tested recipes within your cooking skills. If you want a simple beginning meal, you might consider a brunch. Brunches are nice because breakfast foods are hard to ruin, and even a beginning hostess can make a wonderful brunch at an affordable price.

My first dinner efforts were simple, but they worked. At first, I was not content with any menu I chose because I always felt as though I had not made enough food. That was when I decided to serve taco salad, french bread, and a dessert—every time—until I began to feel comfortable entertaining. After a while, our friends knew immediately what the menu would be—taco salad—but luckily, we loved taco salad enough to eat it often. I could almost prepare it the day before, so I wasn't worn out when the guests arrived. Also, I could afford it.

You'll see why I chose taco salad when you consider its simple recipe:

Combine in large bowl:
1½ heads lettuce
2 tomatoes
1 can drained pinto or kidney beans
1 can drained black olives

Add these next ingredients right before serving:
1 pound cooked hamburger, drained
1½ cups cheese, cubed
1 bag crushed tortilla chips

Top with a house dressing. Serve immediately.
This recipe serves six hearty appetites.

My simplistic approach to getting over the entertaining jitters did produce results. I learned that folks can have a good time together with even a very simple meal. Later on, I felt confident enough to try a different menu.

Invite the right company for your family. A congenial atmosphere must prevail if entertaining is to be a success. If you are a little tense, invite someone who is a lot of fun to be around. Or invite someone who likes to play games afterward. You and your family will get a great deal of satisfaction if you invite someone from a local nursing home or a person who lives alone in your neighborhood. The time will be a success because your guest will most likely appreciate the invitation.

Stay within your budget. Decide what your budget will be and stay within that amount. You will feel a lot better if you avoid overspending. Inviting one couple over and being able to afford it is better than inviting too many people and worrying about a financial strain.

If your budget is really tight now, you could try what my husband and I did when we were first married. We would call up someone and ask them to bring their dinner over and combine it with ours. No extra expense was involved, and it was fun— especially when it was done on the spur-of-the-moment. Sometimes combinations were humorous, yet the company was always great.

Plan like a pro. I decided one day recently that I wanted to visit someone who was a natural hostess so I could learn some of her entertaining secrets. My family knew that our neighbor, Fawn, was a wonderful hostess. I asked Fawn if she would share some of her insights about home entertaining, and she was delighted to have me visit. When I arrived at Fawn's home that evening, Ron, Fawn's husband, was also there and willing to share his own ideas.

Ron and Fawn are in their late thirties. They are gifted entertainers, and they both get involved in the process. They spread their enthusiasm about entertaining by opening their home to bring enjoyment to the people whom they care about. Ron had this to say about why he entertains: "I just enjoy making people extremely welcome in my home, and I get so much myself by watching people interact with each other." Like her husband, Fawn enjoys entertaining from start to finish. She likes to decorate and plan the menu—she just likes to be creative.

Fawn told of a buffet they host each August. They invite close friends and neighbors. They make it a point to have a wide range of ages to add to the fun. The menu is what they call a "mixed grill"—hot dogs, hamburgers, and chicken. The buffet is potluck, so guests bring a wide variety of salads and desserts.

"I decorate the patio with potted plants and flowers, but I think the people are the main decoration," Fawn said. "One year I bought fresh summer corn to accentuate the season, and I put candles all around the patio. Later, as the evening grew dark, we lit the candles and played games. We had a wonderful time."

Ron is the chef at such functions. "I take care of the outside, and Fawn takes care of the inside," he says. "Men are learning that getting involved in family functions is a lot of fun. Besides, Fawn makes me feel as if I am a great chef."

Fawn follows these six steps for any successful entertainment function:

1. *Begin planning two weeks before the event.* The invitations (if it is a large function) must be sent out no later than ten days in advance. Making the guest list has to be done before anything else so that you will know for how many to plan. Make sure you invite people of all ages so the party will be a festive occasion.

2. *Plan your menu* according to the number of guests and the occasion, staying within your budget. Make a list of the items you'll need.

3. *Plan your decorations.* Make a list of things you will need to set the table or area. Don't forget flowers; they are a beautiful way to decorate. Be creative in designing simple decorations. Remember that people are most important.

4. *Do your shopping.*

5. *Prepare as much food as possible the day before the party.* Clean the vegetables, marinate the meat, make the salads or relish. This will save your energy for the next day and you'll be a more relaxed hostess.

6. *Clean your house thoroughly* several days before the party. Don't try to save much cleaning for the day as you'll need your time and energy for other preparations. The morning of the function, clean lightly: dust the house, clean the bathrooms, and vacuum. If at all possible, set the table that morning.

Add charm through table decorations. On any social occasion, you can add those special, easy touches that let your guests know you are happy they came to your home. You can show this by the way you set your table. A pretty table makes the meal more enjoyable, and it even seems to make the food taste better. Cover the table with a colorful tablecloth. Tablecloths can even consist of certain quilts, spreads, or pieces of fabric; so they need not be terribly expensive. A collection of placemats, napkins, and other accessories allow you to fit table decorations to your mood. We all like to look at arrangements that are coordinated and pleasing to the eye. We also appreciate variety and a departure from the ordinary.

One of the biggest surprises in table decorations is "mixed" table settings. Each place setting is different, unique. This can be not only appropriate but beautiful. The hostess can be as creative as she wants to be.

DIFFERENT WAYS TO ENTERTAIN

Nowadays, you can do things most any way you choose. But I feel more comfortable knowing a few basic guidelines before I begin.

Teas and receptions at home. Teas are one of the easiest and loveliest ways to entertain. The menu can include cookies, small cakes, small fancy sandwiches, nuts, tea, and coffee. The tea sits at one end of the table and the coffee sits at the other. When punch is added to a reception, tea is usually omitted. The hostess serves the tea and the guests help themselves to the food. Here is a simple diagram of how to set a table for a tea or reception.

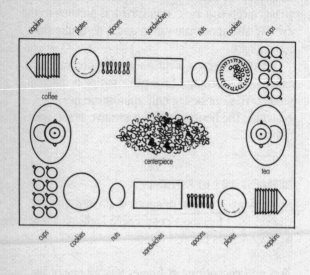

napkins plates spoons sandwiches nuts cookies cups

coffee

centerpiece

tea

cups cookies nuts sandwiches spoons plates napkins

Buffets. Buffets are an informal, comfortable way of entertaining. Except for the dessert, the food goes on the table all at once. The silverware, napkins, and plates are arranged for easy self-serving. To guests this type of entertaining appears easy, but it does take some special planning. The setting of the table should follow a logical sequence. Place the dinner plates and the main dish at one end of the table. Place the other dishes and the table service along the edge of the table for easy access. If the table is too crowded, the beverage can be served from a nearby table or cart. Following is a diagram of two buffet setups.

ONE-LINE BUFFET

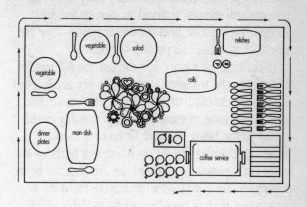

BUFFET WITH BEVERAGE CART

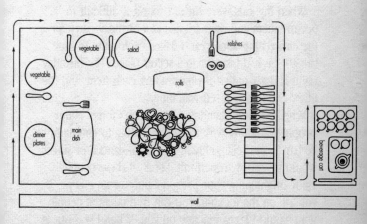

Parties. Parties can be grand whether they are a large gathering or a small family birthday party. They can take national themes, seasonal themes, or holiday themes. They can be held outside or inside. They can celebrate an event or a person—or both!

To decorate for a party, you can use the old standby of balloons and streamers, or make homemade banners using large cut-out letters for a special message. Use your imagination to show off your personality or that of the person being honored. One of my most memorable parties was on my fourteenth birthday. My older sister planned a splendid day. We began at home for dinner. Then we took a hay wagon drawn by ponies to a friend's house for a taffy pull. Later, the party moved to my sister's home for a scavenger hunt. Last of all, we rode home in the wagon for cake and ice cream.

When my kids were little, I found it difficult to occupy them and their friends at a birthday party for the entire time. One year, I asked each child to hide the gift he had brought in a secret place. The birthday child had a wonderful time finding each item, and the other children enjoyed watching.

When you are planning a party, don't forget about people you know who might be willing to entertain. Perhaps a musician, clown, magician, dancer, or singer would be happy to perform. Some of these people enjoy brightening your party for little or no charge. If you are on the lookout, you can find talented people who would like to practice on you. When I was out at a shopping mall, I met a wonderful pianist practicing at a music store. He loves going places to share his talent. Since he is retired, he enjoys the company.

Formal dinners. Our way of living is more casual these days, but I think there is still a place for formal dinners, especially in the family. My children love special occasions, and they get a chance to practice their table manners. One of the children can even act as "maid" or "butler" for added elegance.

The following drawings show how to set the table for each course in a formal dinner. (1) Appetizer: Set the table with a napkin and all the silverware and glassware needed for the rest of the meal. Provide a seafood fork if appropriate. Set the appetizer on an underliner plate. (2) Soup: Provide a soup spoon. Set the soup bowl on an underliner. This course may be omitted, especially if an appetizer is served. (3) Entree: Set each place with a dinner plate, salad plate*, bread-and-butter plate*, table knife, table fork, salad fork*, bread-and-butter knife, and spoon. Provide a glass for each beverage. (4) Dessert: Serve the dessert from the kitchen with the appropriate silverware. Coffee can be served at the table now or later in the living room.

*optional

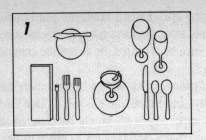

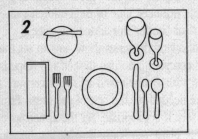

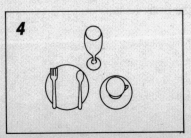

Take some time for yourself. As the hostess, you should wear something comfortable, and something you feel good in. If you look nice, you will feel your best. Make sure your shoes won't hurt your feet and your clothes won't restrict your movement. Casual is often appropriate.

Before the occasion begins, take some time to relax. Try lying down for twenty minutes before the guests arrive. This quiet time of relaxation can make the difference between a harried hostess and a calm, pleasant hostess. Remember: the idea of entertaining is to enjoy yourself and your guests, so make time beforehand to refresh yourself so that you too will have a good time.

▶CHAPTER AT A GLANCE
1. Decide on a no-fail menu.
2. Invite the right company for your family.
3. Stay within your budget.
4. Plan like a pro.
    a. Begin planning two weeks before the event.
    b. Plan your menu.
    c. Plan your decorations.
    d. Do your shopping.
    e. Prepare as much food as possible the day before the party.
    f. Clean your house thoroughly.
5. Add charm through table decorations.

6. Different ways to entertain:
   a. teas and receptions
   b. buffets
   c. parties
   d. formal dinners
7. Take some time for yourself.

ELEVEN
Enjoying Christmas

When you think of Christmas, what do you think of?
Decorated sugar cookies? Excitement in a child's eyes?
Family closeness? Sharing love through a gift
exchange? Christ's special gift of himself?

Or do you think of chaos, financial stress, and
exhaustion? Do you wish Christmas would end as soon
as possible? Do you dread a feeling that the family
closeness wasn't as it should have been and that
maybe exchanging gifts was motivated by obligation
rather than by caring?

If you have experienced both the enchantment and
the exhaustion of Christmas, you share these feelings
with many other women. One woman shared this with
me: "I want to do so many things for my family at
Christmas. I want everything to be perfect. But it
seems that when Christmas is over, my nerves are shot.
The best Christmas present I could ever have would
be to enjoy Christmas myself for a change."

I understand her feelings of frustration. I was at the same place several years ago. I knew that I had to come to some decisions about Christmas.

Decide what you really want Christmas to be. I asked myself some important questions. Was the way we celebrated Christmas what my family really wanted? Was I expecting too much? If our family decided to make some changes, would our parents be hurt or upset? Could I enjoy Christmas myself and still bring enjoyment to my family? What did I really want anyway?

I decided to answer that last question in specific terms. These five things are essential to me:

1. *I want to truly enjoy the holiday myself.* Why? The person who plans any event sets the tone for the other participants. If I am tense and pretending to enjoy Christmas, my children might learn to go through the motions of celebrating Christ's birth with no real meaning. Worship must come from the heart.

2. *I want the family to feel the essence of what Christmas represents: love.* Opportunities to express love can happen only if the atmosphere is conducive to sharing. Especially at Christmastime, love can get lost easily if the pace becomes too hectic. I want to be sure our family doesn't lose the purpose of the holiday because we are too concerned about material objects to care about people.

3. *I want the children to have good memories of hassle-free Christmases.* I feel this will help set the tone by which they pattern their lives in all areas. I

want them to be involved in solving the Christmas pressures creatively.

4. *I want to share with people outside of my family at Christmas.* If I am too tired, I can't share the many blessings I have with others who don't have as much. Christmas can be an extremely lonely time for some folks, and they need a little cheer from people who have it to give. Sharing takes time and energy.

5. *I want simple gratitude to abound within the family on Christmas Day.* It is just too easy to say thank you for a gift when your mind is already on the next gift. I want the Christmas meal to be a family celebration which is not diminished because of the morning gift exchange.

Was I expecting too much? No! I found that I could actually have all five of these things the very first Christmas we made our changes. The first thing our family did was to have a meeting. I shared everything that was on my mind. I kept it very light and asked them if they would like to try something new the next Christmas. We were all a little nervous about making changes, but we decided to give it a try.

A wonderful thing happened that year, and it has happened every year since then: we began to think more creatively so that each year the holiday was a little different. We retained some traditions and added new ones, too. The freedom to be creative brought a fresh enjoyment and excitement to our festivities.

I hesitate to tell you what our first Christmas was like because our friends and relatives felt we had taken Christmas out of Christmas. But our family's flexibility helped us have the courage to be different. One change I wanted involved opening gifts. I wanted each person to be thanked properly. I felt that if I tried to enforce some kind of law mandating gratefulness or love for Christ's birth and for each other, I had already lost the battle. But I did want to take the focus off of the gifts and put it back onto the person who gave the gift.

So that first year, our family began a tradition that we have repeated each year since then. We voted on what kind of gift exchange we wanted: Would it be presents or money? We voted on giving money. A week before Christmas, each child was given fifty dollars to buy their own gifts before and after Christmas— whenever they found the desired item. The second year, we voted on giving gifts, and since that time, the vote for money has been about every other year. Whether we choose money or presents, we still stuff the stockings, and the children buy gifts for each other.

Our first Christmas, I was a little worried about what would happen Christmas morning. Would the children feel let down? The week before Christmas they were constantly on the phone to locate sales for their wanted items. They felt a great sense of accomplishment when they were able to find some items marked down to half price. Their friends on the block were amazed and envious that our children were enjoying new items each day. It seemed as if Christmas Day lasted an entire week.

Christmas morning did come, and I was watching for signs of disappointment. But there were none. Something happened that morning that had never happened before. The tone was calm and relaxed. Each child emptied his or her good-sized stocking. They savored each gift, pausing to thank us. They took time to watch their dad and me empty the treasures from our stockings: items they had purchased themselves. They beamed from ear to ear at seeing our pleasure. They kept hugging us and hugging each other. Since they had received some money from relatives in cards that day, they added that money to any remaining money they had and made plans to do some day-after-Christmas shopping. Their happiness seemed complete.

Dinnertime was also different than it had been in previous years. Everyone was involved. The children acted as if it were the best meal they had ever had, and I, the cook, was enjoying the day more than I had anticipated.

You may wonder about the sharing I had wanted to do. Since my days were not overtaxed by the hassle of shopping and wrapping (except for friends and grandparents), we had time Christmas Eve to visit a mentally ill woman, her husband, and her ten-year-old son. Our children were definitely saddened when they saw that the family's home had no tree to cheer it nor gifts to exchange. They were so glad we had brought the boy a gift and had baked cookies. Because we had spent a relaxed, hassle-free Christmas, we had so much to give, and we received so much by giving.

On the years we decide to exchange gifts, I still want our Christmas experience to have the right emphasis. So I allow the children to "peek" at about half their presents. That removes some of that intense anticipation from gift time. I can't keep Christmas secrets anyway, because I get so excited. My peek policy allows me to be the child that I really am, and it allows the children to see how much I enjoy buying for them.

Believe it or not, this peeking has never ruined things. The kids love knowing what they are getting and, of course, I leave a few surprises.

Now that the children are teenagers, they are finding satisfaction in being creative. For instance, last year Mindy wanted to decorate for Christmas starting the day before Thanksgiving. "Why not?" I giggled. "We can do anything we want to do." And we did decorate (all but a few items) the day before Thanksgiving. Spontaneity and flexibility have added to the celebrating, not taken away from it.

Taking the hassle out of Christmas involves many tasks. Here are just a few:

Christmas baking
Planning the holiday wardrobe
Decorating
Gift wrapping
Sending cards/letters
Distributing gifts/baked goods
Planning holiday menus
House care/pet care

Grocery shopping
Scheduling haircuts, perms
Holiday cleaning
Holiday parties
Buying or making gifts
Church functions for Christmas

Here are some helpful pointers for organizing these projects so you don't become a Mrs. Scrooge by Christmas Eve.

Make a list of all the things you want to do for the holidays. What do you want to bake? What cleaning do you want to do before the festivities begin? I make my Christmas shopping list all year long, whenever I think of a desired gift. That way, when the holidays come, I know exactly what I am seeking. Better yet, whenever I can, I buy items as I find them. (See my book *The Woman's Complete Home Organizer* for Christmas charts.) If you find that your Christmas to-do list is too long, put a star by those things that you could not do without and consider eliminating certain items from your list entirely (more about this later).

Make your list at least six weeks before Christmas. Here's why: You need to divide the tasks over the several preceding weeks so you will experience as little fatigue as possible. To divide your tasks into weeks, you merely list the steps you need to do to complete your Christmas to-do list by Christmas Day.

Beginning November 15, here is how it could read:

WEEK 1

Gift shopping (see Christmas shopping list).
Bake fruitcakes, make shopping list for all baked goods.
Buy Christmas cards, stamps, giftwraps, etc.
Plan Christmas party—guest list, menu, shopping needs.
Schedule hair appointments.
Buy materials for handmade crafts.*

*Note: If you are giving handmade items, you will need to begin these items around the first part of October, especially if your list of projects is extensive.

WEEK 2

Continue gift shopping.
Begin addressing Christmas cards.
Continue making handmade crafts.
Clean oven.
Plan holiday wardrobe.

WEEK 3

Finish Christmas cards and mail them.
Finish gift shopping.
Wrap all gifts.
Mail out-of-town gifts.
Bake cranberry bread and freeze.
Buy holiday clothing.
Decorate house.

WEEK 4

Buy tree and decorate it.
Do last-minute, miscellaneous shopping.
Finish handmade items and wrap.
Bake cookies that freeze well.

WEEK 5

Buy holiday groceries.
Complete house decorating.
Finish housecleaning.
Distribute gifts and baked goods to neighbors and friends.
Relax and enjoy the festivities.

WEEK 6

Relax and visit with the family.
Visit those who need Christmas cheer.
Buy items for Christmas Eve and Christmas Day meals.

Involve your family in the Christmas planning. If
you never have discussed the things your family feels
are important to do at Christmas, you may be
surprised at what you learn. I found my family didn't
require nearly as much as I did for a successful
holiday. If you find you have too much to do in a
given week, ask how they would feel if you eliminated the task completely. You may find that they
wouldn't even miss it, or they may volunteer to do it
themselves.

Involve your family in the actual Christmas preparation. Older children can do so much if you just ask. They will feel like a valuable part of the team in the process. One Christmas (we had voted on a gift exchange), we needed an official gift wrapper. Sixteen-year-old Mindy volunteered. She kept all of the gift wrap, ribbon, tape, and tags in her upstairs bedroom and took charge of this entire operation. All of us simply dropped off our presents with the necessary information. She did the rest. Since she has an artistic flair, she received a lot of compliments for her beautiful job. She felt good about her contribution to the family, and I felt great about not having to worry about all of that.

One Christmas the children took charge of the cut-out sugar cookies. Since they were home from school and I was busy at work, they mixed, rolled, cut out, and baked dozens of cookies. The next evening all three children joined me in frosting and decorating them. Later, the children distributed the cookies to neighbors and friends. That was one time-consuming Christmas task off my list.

Eliminate anything that will take away your personal enjoyment. Pat Cramer is a hardworking homemaker, but she has learned to let some things go. "I used to believe that Christmas had to be perfect. But then I discovered there is really no such thing as perfect. I'm learning to let some things go so I can enjoy the holidays myself. I never thought I would see the day when I would be ordering my Christmas baked goods from the bakery. But I'm doing just that this year, and I feel great about it."

Eliminate, substitute, delegate, or do anything necessary to keep time free so you can relax and enjoy yourself and your family during the holidays. If you begin feeling tense or tired, don't feel as if you must do all that is on your list. Simply decide what things can be eliminated and then do just that. You are only human, and the best gift you can give your family is a mother who is fun to be with and with whom they can share holiday pleasure.

By the way, when it comes to eliminating things, don't be afraid to hire some things done. Christmas comes only once a year; so if you want some cleaning done, go shopping and let your hired help busy themselves with your work. I have always motivated my children and even the neighbor's children to do tasks for a certain amount of money. The children do the tasks that take the time I would rather give to a fun outing with the family or even to myself.

Take time to evaluate how things went this Christmas. Keep a folder of all you did this year to make Christmas planning next year twice as easy. Make a list of things you want to change. While the holiday excitement is still fresh, ask your family what they liked best and what they would like to change next year. Gift wrapping and Christmas decorations are on sale after Christmas, so buy a few things to help prepare for the next year. This will save you time and money.

Remember, the goal of Christmas should be enjoyment for your family and for you, so make a commitment to make sure everyone experiences just that this next holiday season. Plan ahead. Take time for yourself, and don't let anything take away from Christmas. Don't be afraid to be creative and even a little different. Your family will enjoy the holiday more as they watch you having a good time. They will love celebrating God's love with you because Christmas is as it should be: enchanting.

➡CHAPTER AT A GLANCE

1. Decide what you really want Christmas to be.
2. Make a list of all the things you want to do for the holidays.
3. Involve your family in the Christmas planning.
4. Involve your family in the actual Christmas preparations.
5. Eliminate anything that will take away your personal enjoyment.
6. Take time to evaluate how things went this Christmas.

TWELVE
Decorating to Lift Family Spirits

Your home is a place to feel comfortable, to find solace, to relax from the pressures of daily living. The way your home looks affects your mood. Surrounding yourself with things you like and cherish helps make a house a real home. We could get along with only the bare necessities of food, shelter, and clothing. But we have a natural desire to express our personalities in the way we decorate our homes.

Hassles can be caused by boredom and nervous tension. Have you ever noticed how easily bored children get into arguments with each other? We face many pressures at school and at work, so the home environment should be as pleasing as possible to help lift each family member's spirit when he arrives home at the end of the day.

No matter what your budget, home decorating can be lots of fun. If your budget is limited, it will take longer to accomplish your plans, but the end result will be all the more satisfying. Planning doesn't cost any money, and the whole family can get involved. Then, as each small change is added, the family will see the plan take shape.

I have gathered a few pointers from books and interviews to help any woman who wants to make some changes in her home decor. These steps can save you money because you'll avoid making decorating mistakes and buying things you will later regret. They will help you clarify what things you like so that when you decorate a room you won't soon tire of it or even hate it altogether.

Know yourself—your likes, your needs, your personality, your life-style. This sounds easy, but it takes some research to know what you really like. The first time I bought carpet, I made a terrible choice on the spur of the moment. I wanted something that wouldn't show the dirt, and I got that all right. But I also got a mixture of colors I soon hated and that wouldn't go with other things I liked. I had to live with that carpet for years before we moved.

Begin a scrapbook of ideas. Use the library, community college, local bookstores, and furniture decorating classes as resources for gathering information. Cut out pictures in magazines that catch your eye, and keep them in a scrapbook as you try to find a pattern of your preferences. If you like to take pictures, take some of special furniture settings, color schemes at your local furniture store, or your friends' homes. Ask the members of your family for their preferences, because the more input you get, the more valuable your research. Keep all these in your scrapbook.

Choose a particular style. One interior decorator says there are four basic styles nowadays: *Modern Contemporary,* which has the straight, clean lines; *Traditional,* which includes French, Country French, and Italian; *Transitional,* which is not modern, yet has straighter lines than Traditional; and *Early American.*

Choose a color scheme. One idea to help you decide on your favorite colors is to look in your personal wardrobe to find indications of what you like. When I looked in my closet, I found four white blouses, a white jacket, a white sweater, and a white vest. I found I also like earthtone colors and bright accessories. These colors were clues to my decorating preferences.

Remember that color is the basis for all decorating. Certain colors say certain things. Yellow speaks of warmth and cheer. Blue is more cool and formal. Color can beautify a room and set a mood. It makes a room appear larger or smaller. Since there are more than two thousand different colors, a local paint store or art store could help you choose a color scheme. I was surprised to find that yellow can have either a blue base or a yellow base. This is true for any color, and if the two bases are mixed in one room, a displeasing effect will result. Color also has different effects with different lighting. It may be prudent to paint only one wall and observe it in natural light and in artificial light before you paint the entire room.

Decide on a floor plan. Making a floor plan to scale enables you to purchase the right sizes of furniture for your room. To make a floor plan, follow the instructions below.

Purchase several sheets of graph paper (scale: ¼ inch = 1 foot) at your local art supply or craft store. With a ballpoint pen or marking pencil, mark off the dimensions of your room(s) on the graph paper. Using the symbols in chart A as a guide, draw in all permanent features such as doors, windows, fireplaces, radiators, electrical outlets, and any other elements that may affect your plan. Next, photocopy or trace the furniture pieces from chart B and cut out those you need for each room. Experiment freely to choose the most attractive and functional arrangement. The result is a well-balanced room plan without moving heavy furniture.

Make a long-range decorating plan. Most people can't buy everything needed to decorate an entire room or house at one time. When money is limited, you can coordinate your decorating efforts over time by making a long-range plan. You may want to open a savings account for decorating and set aside five or ten dollars each month. Plan to complete one room at a time instead of having several partially finished rooms.

As you plan, think about the theme or mood you want to develop. Do you want formal or informal? Does the room call for certain activities? What are the

Use these typical symbols on the
graph as a guide in planning your rooms.

Base Outlet   Wall Outlet

Ceiling Light   Telephone   Radiator

Double-Hung Window   Window,
                       Open In or Out

Door, Swing In or Out   Arched Opening

SCALE: ¼″ = 1′

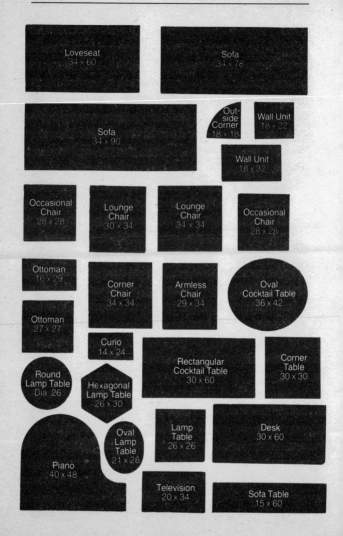

Loveseat
34 x 60

Sofa
34 x 78

Sofa
34 x 90

Outside Corner
18 x 18

Wall Unit
18 x 22

Wall Unit
18 x 32

Occasional Chair
28 x 28

Lounge Chair
30 x 34

Lounge Chair
34 x 34

Occasional Chair
28 x 28

Ottoman
16 x 29

Corner Chair
34 x 34

Armless Chair
29 x 34

Oval Cocktail Table
36 x 42

Ottoman
27 x 27

Curio
14 x 24

Rectangular Cocktail Table
30 x 60

Corner Table
30 x 30

Round Lamp Table
Dia. 26

Hexagonal Lamp Table
26 x 30

Oval Lamp Table
21 x 26

Lamp Table
26 x 26

Desk
30 x 60

Piano
40 x 48

Television
20 x 34

Sofa Table
15 x 60

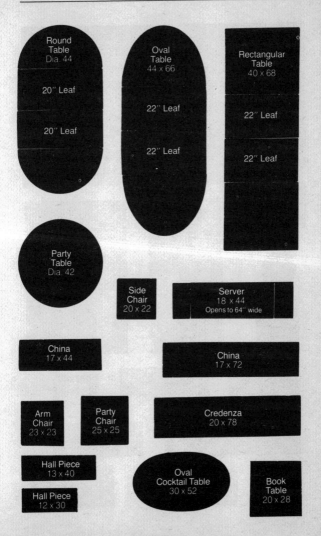

Round Table
Dia. 44

20" Leaf

20" Leaf

Oval Table
44 x 66

22" Leaf

22" Leaf

Rectangular Table
40 x 68

22" Leaf

22" Leaf

Party Table
Dia. 42

Side Chair
20 x 22

Server
18 x 44
Opens to 64" wide

China
17 x 44

China
17 x 72

Arm Chair
23 x 23

Party Chair
25 x 25

Credenza
20 x 78

Hall Piece
13 x 40

Hall Piece
12 x 30

Oval Cocktail Table
30 x 52

Book Table
20 x 28

157

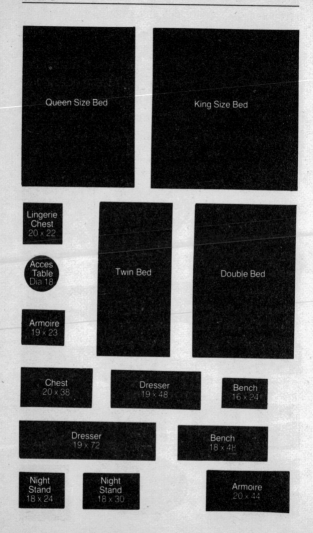

Queen Size Bed

King Size Bed

Lingerie
Chest
20 x 22

Acces
Table
Dia 18

Twin Bed

Double Bed

Armoire
19 x 23

Chest
20 x 38

Dresser
19 x 48

Bench
16 x 24

Dresser
19 x 72

Bench
18 x 48

Night
Stand
18 x 24

Night
Stand
18 x 30

Armoire
20 x 44

needs of your family? Do certain daily activities call for more space or for different kinds of furniture? Consider both beauty and function.

Even with restricted time or finances, you can probably begin some changes right away. Small things like plants add life to your home. A gallon of paint can cost as little as twelve dollars and will usually cover a small room. An investment in a throw pillow, throw rug, lamp, mirror, or picture can be the beginning you need. Be sure to purchase or make only those items that will fit into your overall plan.

You can probably find ways to use many of the things you already have. Fabrics or refinishing can be used to make almost any piece of furniture fit into your decor. For instance, if you have a traditional chair and you want a country look, simply cover the chair in a country fabric. Bring out things you love and cherish for family use. A favorite decoy, silver spoon, or vase can enhance your room now and, for variety, can later be moved from table to mantel to curio.

Evaluate who will do what. Do you plan to do the work yourself? How will the children help? Decorating can be a family affair, although not everyone in the family will have similar ideas. The differences, however, can stimulate change and experimentation. If you hire work out, examine previous work done by the person you hire to make sure he does quality work. Be sure you don't allow someone else to influence your ideas. You, not anyone else, must live with your decor.

Doing your own work will save money, and the results can be very rewarding. Don't be intimidated by your inexperience. If you want to learn to hang wallpaper, for example, check your resources. A friend who has done a good job might lend you a hand, and stores that sell wallpaper offer good advice.

Children can be a resource for living area decorating, and they should also have a say in decorating their rooms. A child's room is his own space, so allow the child to help choose colors, furniture, and fabrics. If the child is very young and likes red, though, he may not know how much red he really likes. Since red is an unrestful color, you may want to use it for trim, accessories, or the bedspread rather than painting the entire room red. Children learn from opportunities to be creative. As children get older, they can take more responsibility for decorating their own rooms. In any case, they will need to make some changes as they mature and their preferences change.

Decorate according to seasons, holidays, or events for added zest. *Seasonal decorating* starts when you take nature walks and then bring nature inside. Bring in sprigs of tree blossoms in the spring, fresh flowers in the summer, and a bouquet of leaves in autumn. During the winter you can bring summer inside by planting a pot of tulips. Or decorate a grapevine wreath according to each season using spring flowers, autumn leaves, or winter evergreens.

Since children love to create, let them take turns

designing a small bulletin board for the kitchen with a few treasures from nature. Such decorating is usually free of charge, and it adds so much zest. You can gather other ideas from local florists.

Holiday decorating adds variety to any home. You can use the fireplace or a special table for such decorating. Make a little scene for each holiday with flowers, ceramics, pictures, or candles. If your living room or dining room has neutral tones, you can remove any throw pillows or tablecloths and add the appropriate colors for the occasion.

When you *decorate for parties,* it is important to decide on a theme. What atmosphere will you create: a Mexican Fiesta, a German Fest, or a child's wonderland? Save decorations from year to year to enhance each occasion.

Remember that decorating depends only on the personality of the decorator. Be as creative as you want to be by buying new things or by using things you already have in new ways. With your personal and creative touch, a room will have an expression all its own and will lift the family's spirits.

▶CHAPTER AT A GLANCE

1. Know yourself.
2. Begin a scrapbook of ideas.
3. Choose a particular style.
4. Choose a color scheme.
5. Decide on a floor plan.

6. Make a long-range decorating plan.
7. Evaluate who will do what.
8. Decorate according to seasons, holidays, or events for added zest.

PART THREE: STOP AND RE-GROUP

THIRTEEN
Taking Time for You

Think about the last time you relaxed totally. For a short time you weren't rushing to get someplace. You weren't fighting the clock at all. You were just enjoying yourself. How long ago was it?

How about now? Are your shoulders tight? Is your breathing shallow? Are you tense? Chances are, you may be. The average woman often finds it difficult to take time to relax and enjoy herself.

Although the general effects of stress have been studied for some time, psychologist Richard Lazarus, Ph.D., and his colleagues at the University of California at Berkeley were among the first to scrutinize the impact of daily hassles on individuals. Over the course of a year, they asked one hundred middle-class, middle-aged men and women to fill out questionnaires including a monthly checklist of 117 common irritations. Hassles in the study included not enough time for the family, losing things, not getting enough rest, and friction with a coworker. Each person checked off the tensions he felt each month, how often they occurred, and how severe the stress had been. He also answered questions about his health. Lazarus and his colleagues found that those who experienced the most hassles had poorer physical and mental health. He wrote, "Daily hassles . . . may have a greater effect on our moods and our health than the major misfortunes of life."

Not only is it helpful to take time out; it is necessary. You must get away from the kids, the dog, the house, and countless obligations once in a while. Taking time out for yourself refreshes your outlook and clears your mind. Everyday hassles have a way of looking a lot worse when you are viewing them close up. When you back up a little, things tend to return to the proper perspective.

The trouble is that many women don't budget time for themselves. Women often feel as if they must be superwomen. They are so busy doing for everybody else they forget they have limited resources. Most women recognize the need to take time out, but finding the time is difficult. To keep up with their many responsibilities, working women often eliminate quality personal time from their schedules. And when they finally do take a little time for themselves, they are too tired to enjoy it.

I always sense when I have allowed my endless projects and duties to squeeze out the time for myself: I am just no fun to be around. My mind is so preoccupied that I lose my sense of humor and become introspective. At those times I remind myself that life is too short not to enjoy it, and my friends and family deserve better.

Recently, an older gentleman who often comes to our home remarked, "There is so much laughter in this home. I feel wonderful here." But sad to say, I too often forget how important it is to relax and take time to enjoy myself. I have noticed that when I have joy, my family responds in kind. More importantly, I find great satisfaction in having fun myself.

You may be saying that you also see the necessity of taking time out for yourself, but it is just not that easy to find the time to do it. If you have small children, you face the problem of needing to hire a baby-sitter, and that costs money. Or, if you have teenage children, you may spend much of your free time acting as chauffeur and performing countless other duties. Your time gets low priority.

But if you don't take care of yourself, who will? If you don't watch out for your mental and physical health, who will?

Just suppose you do have a block of time each week to do whatever you choose. Don't worry yet about when that block of time might occur. Just think for a moment about how you would like to spend it. Consider these four time-out areas.

Take time out for your body. Melinda is twenty-nine and the mother of two young daughters. She finds that regular exercise helps her maintain a positive attitude through difficult times. She is so sold on the benefits of exercise that she not only maintains a regular program herself, she teaches aerobics classes at a local church and at a health club. Her children and her husband are also involved in exercise programs.

Melinda's husband has been out of work for the last two years, and things have not been easy for her family. One day I asked her how she was able to bring such vibrance and enthusiasm to the women in her classes when she was under a lot of pressure.

Her answer surprised me a little: "I know it is hard to believe, but I haven't had any bouts of depression during these last two years, and I know it is simply because I keep active. It just makes me feel good about myself and, actually, I feel the best I have felt in the last ten years."

Melinda tells of a woman who worked at a hospital who did become depressed often. She and her husband were under a tremendous amount of stress. But since this woman began coming to the exercise class, her attitude has changed. She told Melinda, "Exercise has taught me how to laugh again." Melinda says another woman was suffering from tension backaches. Slow stretching has helped her immensely.

Studies have shown that when a person exercises, the body releases endorphins, which have a tranquilizing effect. Of course, exercise affects how you look because it tones your muscles. Your mind and body respond favorably to a regular exercise program. You feel better about yourself. Developing an exercise routine is easier than it has ever been before because you can find exercise groups located in almost every section of town. Park districts usually have a wide selection of classes from which to choose. Many churches are opening their facilities for women's exercise groups. I have found that listening to exercise records help me. The girls and I like doing our routines together at home. It is fun to invite a friend to join you as you exercise, especially if you need a little extra motivation to get into a regular schedule.

Taking time out for your body through exercise is not wasted time. You will feel better about yourself if you feel healthy and attractive. Hassles won't seem as overwhelming and difficult. Don't allow the stress of daily living to keep you from taking care of your body.

Take time out to expand your talents. Every woman has gifts that need cultivation. These abilities are so diverse that we often don't recognize them as gifts. I took a long time to realize that I have the ability to organize. I had done it all my life, organizing seemed quite ordinary. But even though you or I may not be an artist or a musician, the talents we have are important.

My father, who has a gift in woodworking, believes that he will be a craftsman in heaven. Please don't laugh at the prospect. You see, your gifts and abilities are part of your personality, and your personhood will exist forever. When we enter the next life with a new, incorruptible body, we will have a greater magnitude of creative ability. Our abilities are valued so highly by God that he expects us to be good stewards of these gifts and abilities.

Think for a few moments about your own abilities. Are you a good listener? Are you good with money? Do you like to read?

Linda was seeking to use her gifts, but she was unable to discern where her talents actually lay. Then she thought about how much she enjoyed reading. Several days later, she remembered how much she enjoyed old folks. She put the two together: weekly, she would read to older folks in a home for the aged. She found great satisfaction in using these abilities.

Many of our talents must be cultivated and developed. Each step we take can open new avenues. To be fulfilled you must use your gifts and share them with others. You will be surprised when you see just how small hassles appear to a woman who is expanding her abilities. She is too busy to overreact. Her increased confidence, due to the time given to her own talents, makes it easier to deal with problems.

Below write any of your known or suspected talents. These should include things that you just enjoy doing, because the things you enjoy reveal your abilities.

Spend time in meditation. Meditation is not necessarily something you do with a turban on your head with your arms and legs folded. You can meditate anywhere at any time. A valuable devotional exercise would be to look up the many verses in the Bible that

1.

2.

3.

4.

5.

6.

7.

8.

9.

10.

---

speak about meditation. The Psalms especially give many helpful insights.

The other night I went to pick up my daughter and her friends at the stadium after a football game. The game had gone into overtime, and I waited in the car for forty-five minutes. It was a perfect time for meditation. I recounted certain things and thought through some questions I had. When the six giggly teenagers apologized for being late, I told them I was enjoying the solitude and didn't mind the lateness.

Solitude can be planned or unplanned, but either way it can be very refreshing. I often take the car, buy a soda, and sit at a park or church so I can meditate. Sad to say, meditation is almost a lost art in our fast-paced society, and people show the effects of not having this time. We all need it.

My meditation time helps me evaluate how I feel about certain things and what I am going to do about them. This time helps me keep in touch with myself and with the God who made me. Even though I am not actively praying during these times, I am aware of who I am and who I want to become with God's help. I believe God accepts much of my quiet meditations as prayers because much of the time I am enjoying his quiet presence. Often I spend my meditation times just enjoying the creation around me, amazed at how creative God is. I know he appreciates my noticing the talent he so beautifully displays.

Take time to do things you enjoy. Some things don't necessarily improve your health, improve your talents, or fall under the category of meditation, but you like to do them just for the fun of it. When you are having fun, you are more refreshed, and you find it easier to return to and deal with any homemaking hassle. Countless crafts, games, sports, pastimes, or events are simply fun to do. You need these to be a well-rounded, healthy person. So do those things and enjoy them.

If you find that you are unable to "waste" time on yourself, you may want to re-examine how you feel about yourself. Many of us harbor poor self-esteem. We don't feel as if we are worth the time, the money, and the effort. And what about guilt feelings? I have had to overcome both of these, because I felt guilty if I took time away from my family. It seemed so unnecessary and so extravagant. I doubted that I was being responsible. This attitude helped no one; it harmed me as a person.

Right now, prepare to *make a list of things you*

enjoy doing. Would you like to study poetry or history, learn photography, or visit an art gallery? *Make a quick estimate of the expense* that might be involved in some of these interests. For example, photography requires a certain investment and if you can't afford it, you can write it on your list but may have to wait until later to purchase the equipment. Consider buying used equipment or checking out books on the subject at your public library. *Estimate the time you would need* each week to do the activity.

Interests	Expense	Time Needed
1.		
2.		
3.		
4.		
5.		
6.		
7.		
8.		
9.		
10.		

You could probably afford at least two or three things on the above list. Now you must make a decision as to when and in what order you will pursue these interests. If you have small children, you will have to make arrangements for their care while you take time out. Perhaps you and a friend could share in the effort by exchanging child-care times to save on expense. Or hire a sitter. If what you pursue needs to be done in the evening, ask for assistance and support from your husband. Anything you must do is worth the refreshment you will receive as you take time out for yourself.

Last of all, *schedule the time on your calendar.* Block out the time you need and don't let anything interfere. It is my opinion that you will need two hours as a minimum for most activities. Anything less is too short, for just as you begin to relax and enjoy yourself, it's time to come home. Remember: you will be better equipped to handle any hassle on the homefront if you take care of yourself by getting away from it all on a regular basis. And you deserve it.

▶CHAPTER AT A GLANCE

1. Take time out for your body.
2. Take time out to expand your talents.
3. Spend time in meditation.
4. Take time to do things you enjoy.
5. Make a list of things you enjoy doing.
6. Estimate the expense and time involved.
7. Schedule a time and begin.

FOURTEEN
Spending Time
with God

Have you ever made a decision to have a regular time every day with God? Are you convinced that you need to take time out for God, but try as you might, you just have trouble being consistent about spending that time?

Spending time with God is very important. Why? Daily hassles can take the joy out of life if we rely only on our personal resources. We need divine help to keep a positive attitude despite any hassle that comes our way. We know that God is the source of all life and all fulfillment. His plan, in which we all participate, is somewhat beyond our comprehension. Just about the time we get things figured out a little, they change. Too many people have tried to keep their lives together without the true peace and happiness that comes from a relationship with God.

If you are a person committed to Christ, you

recognize that your life is incomplete without the One who designed you. Life's hassles will come and go but your time with God will bring peace to otherwise disastrous days, and give you the divine help you need to overcome.

If you feel inadequate when it comes to spending time with God, then you should know you are not alone. If the truth were known, everyone has trouble in this area.

I will never forget the rejuvenation I felt after hearing a story from Jack Hayford, a very sincere pastor of a large church in Van Nuys, California. Pastor Hayford had a confession to make about his daily devotions. He admitted that on certain days he didn't feel at all like reading the Bible. In fact, he said, on some days he felt about as spiritual as a frog: "On those days, I try to read at least one verse before I go to bed."

Through the years, I have known many pastors and their wives, and I have never met one of these people who did not struggle and fall short of what they felt they should be doing to maintain their walk with God. Teaching from Scripture on the subject of knowing God is one thing. Applying that to your everyday life is another.

Knowing God is a life-long project. To know God, one must, in part, deal with intangibles. As finite beings, we must use our finite, human capacities to relate to a God who is infinite, all powerful, and all knowing.

God is greater than our knowledge of him. We have only to look at the heavens and the earth and we know how very insignificant we would be if God didn't have the ability to attend to great creations and still care about every detail of our lives. He can't be mastered or completely understood because, simply stated, our conceptual capacities are too limited.

We must know ourselves. I'm convinced that a large part of the salvation process involves coming to grips with who we actually are. Once in a while, it seems to dawn on us that we are destined for a day when we will be "unveiled" as sons of God (Rom. 8:19). Most of the time, it is just too hard to understand that when God bought us with his own life, he intended to make us a part of his family. God takes great pleasure in patiently revealing his great love for us. And all the while he knows full well we won't really see it until we actually see him face to face. At that time everything we want to know about our true natures will be revealed to us.

In the meantime, coming to grips with a knowledge of ourselves is extremely important. To know God, one must not only allow God to be God in truth, but one must be willing to be known in truth.

Be yourself before God. No woman can have a fulfilling time with God each day if she tries to be someone other than who she is. She can't pray meaningfully if she is trying to pray as someone else does or as someone says she should. Sometimes I laugh at my prayer efforts in earlier years when I tried to get the formula right. It was difficult to understand that God wanted me to share with him from my heart rather than what I perceived to be the correct formula. Your devotional life must come from you as an individual.

You are different from every other person in the world for a reason. God is so creative that he can make each person unique. Also, we are shaped by experience. No two people have exactly the same background and experiences. Even members of the same family have experiences different from other family members.

When Laura looks at a landscape, she sees the same scenery I do but with completely different insight. I see trees, flowers, and an old barn. She sees multi-shaded, green trees. She sees depth, size comparisons, textures, and the way the light reflects off certain portions of the landscape.

My husband looks at things from a scientific viewpoint. He becomes completely overwhelmed when he notes scientific facts about the stars. He talks about light-years, supernovas, and neutron stars, those highly compact bodies that, per cubic inch, could easily weigh 1.8 million million tons. Quite frankly, some of these things are beyond me.

If I didn't understand that I am a different person from people around me, I might try to modify my relationship with God to fit my neighbor's. In the process, I would lose something very valuable: my own friendship with God.

Be who you are and offer that to God in your daily devotions. He made you the way you are and *likes* you the way you are.

PRAYER

If you are wanting to improve your prayer life, you would do well to simply look up all the Bible references on the subject. As you do, I believe you will notice the following things.

Prayer can be done at any time during the day. Daniel prayed in the morning, late at night, or sometimes during the day. David prayed similarly. The time of day you pray is up to you. No hard-and-fast rule is recorded in the Bible, only examples of different people's preferences.

Prayer can be done in any physical posture. Christ often prayed as he walked with his disciples (John 17). He prayed seated, standing, kneeling, and in a prone position. King David prayed as he lay in his bed as well as in the above postures. The point is this: Prayer can be done no matter what you are doing or where you are.

Prayer can be long or short. Daniel probably had three short sessions daily. Jesus had short times or long times, depending on the need at hand. Before major tests or after the loss of John the Baptist, for instance, he took considerable time out for prayer.

Regardless of how long you pray each day, you should take into consideration the time you are now spending. If you pray for five minutes daily, and want to increase your time, increase it to ten minutes. If you try to go from five minutes to thirty minutes, you will probably fail. An increase of any kind should always be considered a success.

Pray about anything and everything. If you want to see an honest prayer life from someone God considered to be after his own heart, look at the psalms David prayed. David was very honest with God. He told him exactly how he felt, and told him what he wanted. He expressed anger over his enemies (can you imagine that?). He even complained if he thought God was waiting too long to answer him. He told God how afraid he was. There were no secrets between David and God.

Most of us could learn from David's example. It is very hard to get answers to prayers if you neglect to tell God you have a need. I have found that telling God everything is one way I rid myself of anxiety. When I feel nervous, I talk to God—describing every little detail. I used to believe this was not necessary since God knows everything already. However, he loves to have us share every detail. And when we do, he shares his insight and his peace.

If you find yourself at a loss for words when you take time out to pray, you should know that this is a perfectly normal human experience. Romans 8:26 says, "We know not what we should pray for as we ought: but the Spirit himself maketh intercession for us."

Getting to know anyone, including God, takes time. The time you spend can differ from one day to another. Sometimes you may feel like acting silly; the next time you may be quiet. Sometimes you may be extremely talkative and outgoing, while at other times you would rather be reflective.

In your time with God, it may help you if you talk to God just like you talk with someone with whom you feel comfortable. Share how your day is going. Share good or bad events. Share the things that are on your mind, concerns and worries. And if you don't feel like talking to God, come anyway. Some of the most meaningful, tender times I have ever spent with God were silent times. You may want to say something like this: "I don't feel like talking now. I just come to you because I want to be with you; I need you. I come to you because I know today that you are the Source of my life. I am just going to sit here in your presence because I love you."

Really, God doesn't care how eloquent you are. He just loves to be with you. When he entered into history and became the God-Man for all eternity, he emptied himself to give himself to you and me. Once and for all, that proved his desire to have us in his presence. He loved us so much he gave himself. It isn't really much more complicated than that.

As you take time out for God each day, it may help you to be a little creative. Do things a little differently to maintain interest. Maybe you should change the location of your prayer time or maybe change your approach. Whatever you do, be the person you are and share honestly from your heart.

SCRIPTURE READING

Scripture reading is a valuable part of the devotional time. The Bible is not always easy to understand, however. Still, a little investigation can turn up some valuable tools to help you understand the Bible more clearly. One such tool, which I have found very helpful, is a book entitled *Protestant Biblical Interpretation* by Bernard Ramm. I'm sure your pastor or church librarian can recommend other books on biblical interpretation. There are also many fine Bible-study guides to help you understand different subjects or portions of Scripture. These can assist you in maintaining interest in Scripture reading.

No matter how much one understands the Bible, it is still easy to neglect it and leave it for days before picking it up again. Everyone has done it, including me. But here are some ways I maintain interest in my Scripture-reading schedule.

Give yourself a relaxed reading schedule. I don't insist that I read a certain amount each day. Rather, I look at my schedule and decide on certain days that I am going to spend the afternoon curled on the couch reading. Other days, I read only a few verses. If you are someone who does not utilize time very well, this may not work for you. Some people need to make a commitment to read ten minutes per day. I have always been the kind of person who can get a five-minute start on something, leave it because of an interruption, and then come back to it without having lost my train of thought. So your time will need to be tailored to fit you.

I have often benefited from reading one or two verses in the morning so that I can meditate on them while I am at work. I have also found it helpful to not close my Bible on certain days so that I can grab a verse in between activities.

Evelyn, a woman I work with, has her Scripture "reading" as she drives to work each morning. She listens to Bible tapes in the car and says she is able to remember a lot more when she hears it rather than reads it. Some musicians sing the Scriptures, and for that reason we have many beautiful verses put to song. One man I know prays over Scripture. As he reads it, he says a prayer about it. If he is reading about the love of God, he may read the verse to the Father and thank him for his love.

Take advantage of the many Bible translations.
Read through the four Gospels looking for Christ's prayer life in one translation, and then go back through the Gospels in another translation to zero in on the teachings Christ gave on the subject of prayer. Different translations can help a Bible reader see things overlooked before.

As with your prayer times, your Bible reading may come easier if you adapt it to your own needs and use your own creativity. You will find meaning in your daily time with God only if you do it your way. But whatever you do, have patience with your efforts, because all of us are learning in this area. No one has mastered this yet, and that is perfectly all right. We have all eternity to explore the God who made us, and we will never approach him if we don't allow ourselves to be human and in need of growth.

I just love coming to a God who knows me and still loves me. I would never come to a God who demanded perfection. Christ's blood has provided access to the Father, so when you take time out for God, be yourself, be creative, and persist in spite of everything. The reward is knowing God, and knowing him will bring you peace and happiness regardless of how many hassles may come your way.

▶CHAPTER AT A GLANCE
1. Spending time with God is very important.
2. Knowing God is a life-long project.
3. We must know ourselves.
4. Be yourself before God.
5. Prayer can be done at any time during the day.
6. Prayer can be done in any physical posture.
7. Prayer can be long or short.
8. Pray about anything and everything.
9. Give yourself a relaxed reading schedule.
10. Take advantage of the many Bible translations.

THE 30-DAY MENU CHART (Not to be used in consecutive order)

1   Simple Quiche
    Toast
    Fruit cup

2   Pepper steak
    Rice
    Peas
    Sliced oranges

*3 Beef vegetable soup
    Crackers
    Oatmeal cake

4   Macaroni and cheese
    Peas
    Fruit cup

*5   Chicken soup
      Crackers
      Applesauce
      Cookies

6   Barbecued chicken
    Baked potatoes
    Cooked carrots
    Fruit bowl

7   Frozen prepared chicken
    Scalloped potatoes
    Green beans
    Fruit bowl

8   Baked chicken
    Baked potatoes
    Tossed green salad
    Yogurt

9   Meat loaf
    Baked potatoes
    Mixed vegetables
    Fruit bowl

10   Swedish meatballs
    Rice
    Peas and carrots
    Sliced apples

11   Tacos
    Yogurt and strawberries

12   Sloppy Joes
    Sourdough buns
    Celery and carrot sticks
    Orange slices

13   Chili con carne
     Corn bread
     Pear slices

---

14   Spaghetti
     Tossed green salad
     Bread (optional)
     Fruit bowl

---

15   Baked ham and pineapple
     Biscuits
     Peas
     Carrot sticks
     Pudding

---

16   Ham and cheese casserole
     Toast
     Carrot salad

---

17   Ham and eggs
     Waffles
     Applesauce

---

18   Fish fillets
     Scalloped potatoes
     Cooked cabbage
     Fruit cup

---

19   Pork chops
     Dressing
     Broccoli casserole
     Applesauce

---

20   Veal or beef patties
     Broccoli
     Baked potatoes
     Peaches

21 Grilled cheese sandwiches
   Tomato soup
   Fruit salad

22 Bacon, lettuce, and tomato sandwiches
   Cottage cheese and fruit

23 Wieners and sauerkraut
   Peas
   Bread and butter
   Pudding

24 Hamburgers
   Tater Tots
   Fruit bowl

25 Clam chowder
   Cheese and crackers
   Vegie tray
   Dip

26 Hot dogs
   French fries
   Carrot sticks
   Fruit bowl

27 Taco salad
   Pudding with whipped cream

28 Toast treats
   Celery and peanut butter
   Fruit salad

29 Pizza
   Tossed green salad
   Fruit bowl

30 Refried beans and cheese
    Taco chips
    Tossed green salad
    Fruit bowl

ALSO AVAILABLE FROM THE AUTHOR:

The Complete Photo Album Accessory—to help you organize your family pictures. $6.50.

The Woman's Complete Calendar/Organizer—with complete charts for organizing every aspect of your busy life. $12.50.

To order, send check or money order to:

RENA STRONACH
Post Office Box 2574
Eugene, Oregon 97402
Phone: 503/683-2632

Other Living Books Best-sellers

ROOM FOR ONE MORE by Nyla Booth and Ann Scott. Ann and Phil Scott, with two daughters of their own, found themselves adopting not one, but eventually fifteen needy children. A heartwarming true story. 07-5711 $3.50.

SUSANNA by Glen Williamson. Meet Susanna Wesley, the mother of John and Charles Wesley, a most unusual though lesser-known woman of Christian history. This stirring testimony will challenge Christians to establish a strong foundation of faith for their children. 07-6691 $3.50.

LORD, COULD YOU HURRY A LITTLE? by Ruth Harms Calkin. These prayer-poems from the heart of a godly woman trace the inner workings of the heart, following the rhythms of the day and the seasons of the year with expectation and love. 07-3816 $2.95.

BITTERSWEET LOVE by Betty R. Headapohl. In this touching romance, Trevor, a wealthy land developer, falls in love with Starr, a health food store owner. Then Starr's former fiancé reappears, and the sparks start to fly. 07-0181 $3.50.

HUNTED GUN by Bernard Palmer. Colorado rancher John Breck encounters an ambush, suspicious townspeople, and deceit spawned by gold fever in this fast-paced yet thoughtful western for adults. 07-1497 $3.50.

HER CONTRARY HEART by Lois T. Henderson. A fascinating historical romance revealing the inner turbulence of a young and spirited woman who questions the tenets of the strict Harmonist Society to which she belongs. 07-1401 $3.95.

SUCCESS: THE GLENN BLAND METHOD by Glenn Bland. The author shows how to set goals and make plans that really work. His ingredients of success include spiritual, financial, educational, and recreational balances. 07-6689 $3.50.

KAREN'S CHOICE by Janice Hermansen. College students Karen and Jon fall in love and are heading toward marriage when Karen discovers she is pregnant. Struggle with Karen and Jon through the choices they make and observe how they cope with the consequences and eventually find the forgiveness of Christ. 07-2027 $2.95.

LET ME BE A WOMAN by Elisabeth Elliot. In these days of conflicting demands and cultural pressures, what kind of woman do you wish to be? With profound and moving insights, this best-selling author presents her unique perspective of womanhood. 07-2162 $3.95.

RAISING CHILDREN by Linda Raney Wright. Twelve well-known Christian mothers give their views on parenthood, sharing insights and personal experiences from family life that will both amuse you and cause you to think. 07-5136 $2.95.

The books listed are available at your bookstore. If unavailable, send check with order to cover retail price plus $1.00 per book for postage and handling to:

Christian Book Service
Box 80
Wheaton, Illinois 60189

Prices and availability subject to change without notice. Allow 4–6 weeks for delivery.